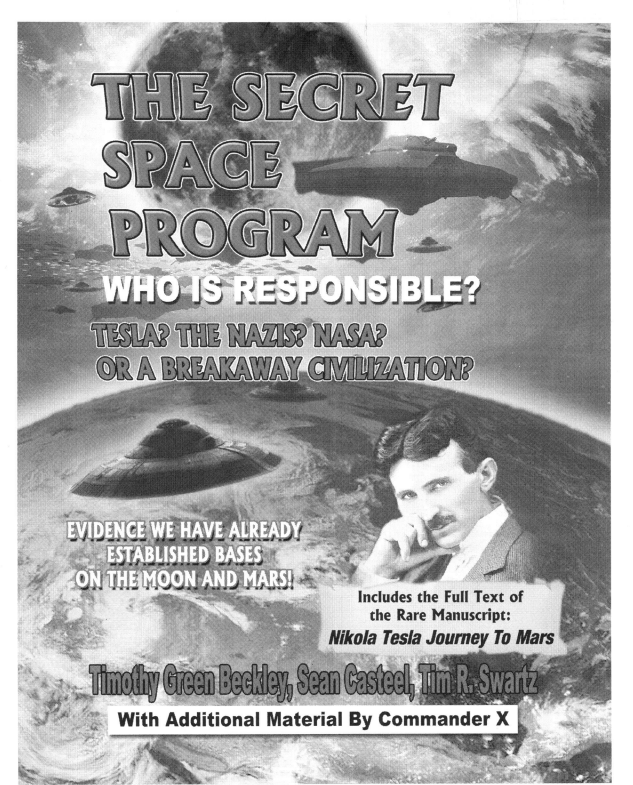

THE SECRET SPACE PROGRAM

WHO IS RESPONSIBLE?

TESLA? THE NAZIS? NASA? OR A BREAKAWAY CIVILIZATION?

EVIDENCE WE HAVE ALREADY ESTABLISHED BASES ON THE MOON AND MARS!

Includes the Full Text of
the Rare Manuscript:
Nikola Tesla Journey To Mars

Timothy Green Beckley, Sean Casteel, Tim R. Swartz

With Additional Material By Commander X

Global Communications

The Secret Space Program

By Timothy Green Beckley
Sean Casteel, Tim R. Swartz
and Commander X

Timothy Green Beckley: Editorial Director
Carol Rodriguez: Publisher's Assistant
Sean Casteel: Associate Editor
Cover Art: Tim Swartz

Printed in the United States of America
For free catalog write:
Global Communications
P.O. Box 753
New Brunswick, NJ 08903

Free Subscription to Conspiracy Journal E-Mail Newsletter
www.conspiracyjournal.com

CONTENTS

From The Earth To The Moon And Beyond --
Exposing An Invisible Empire .... - 9 -

Mysterious Triangles And A Breakaway Civilization .... - 13 -

Why Believe In A Secret Space Program? ....- 13 -

What About Mars? ....- 15 -

The Breakaway Civilization ....- 16 -

The 'Sophisticated' Nazis ....- 17 -

So Who Is Running The Show? ....- 19 -

Dominating Space ....- 20 -

Who In Government Knows About All This? ....- 21 -

Responding To The Alien Presence ....- 22 -

Would That Include Triangle Ships? ....- 23 -

The Cash-Landrum Incident ....- 24 -

What We Know And What We Don't Know ....- 24 -

The Martian Eye In The Sky Has Always
Been Looking Down On Us! .... - 27 -

A Little Later On ....- 30 -

Is There A Secret Et Presence On The Moon And Mars? .... - 33 -

Too Contrived? ....- 34 -

Civilizations On Mars ....- 36 -

Did Nikita Khrushchev Try To Set Up Shop On The Moon? .... - 39 -

Space Bases – You Can Blame Them On Hitler! .... - 45 -
The Story Of Iron Sky .... - 45 -
The Stuff Of Legends .... - 47 -
The Accusations Fly .... - 48 -
Hitler Under The Influence .... - 49 -
Where Did This Knowledge Come From? .... - 50 -
The Beautiful Mediums Of The Vril .... - 52 -

The Bedazzling Claims Of A Hacker .... - 55 -
What Did He Actually Find? .... - 56 -
In The Interest Of 'Disclosure' .... - 57 -
A Therapist Provides Confirmation .... - 58 -

Nasa's Magickal Mystery Tour .... - 61 -
Jack Parsons, An Unlikely Space Age Pioneer .... - 61 -
Blowing Things Up .... - 62 -
A Little Evil On The Side .... - 64 -
A Legacy Of Rumor And Strangeness .... - 66 -

Bedding Down With The Masons On The Moon .... - 69 -
Marrs On The Masons .... - 70 -

Richard Hoagland: Whistle Blower Or Master Of Deception? .... - 75 -
Photographic Evidence .... - 76 -
Structures On The Moon .... - 77 -
More Conspiracy Claims .... - 77 -

Heil To The Men From Mars! Outreach And Diplomatic Relations ... - 79 -
A Diplomatic Outreach From Mars .... - 79 -
Signs Of Life On Mars .... - 81 -
Did The Martians Colonize Earth? .... - 82 -

A Martian Wanderer – The Astounding Claims Of President Eisenhower's Great-Granddaughter... - 85 -

Multi-Dimensions.. - 87 -

Encountering Attacks .... - 88 -

The Roots Of The Ancient Game .... - 89 -

Nowhere To Run .... - 90 -

Meeting Agent X And The Mars Mission .... - 91 -

Refusing To Go To Mars .... - 94 -

Where Do We Go From Here? .... - 98 -

Journey To Mars By Nikola Tesla .... - 99 -

Tesla And The Martian Connection .... - 99 -

Introduction By Commander X .... - 101 -

Chapter 1 Secret Societies Of The 1800's .... - 103 -
The Story Begins .... - 103 -
The Sightings Continue .... - 104 -
Of Human Origin? .... - 105 -
Human Occupants .... - 106 -
Mysterious Scrapbook .... - 109 -
A Secret Society's Airships? .... - 111 -
Negate Weight Or Antigravity Flight .... - 112 -

Chapter 2 Enter The Nazis.................................... - 117 -
Ufos Behind Enemy Lines .... - 117 -
Nazis And The Occult .... - 118 -
Nazis Achieve Results .... - 119 -
The Foo-Fighters .... - 120 -
Bringing It All Back Home .... - 122 -
In Bed With The Nazis.. - 123 -
Playing With The Truth....................................... - 125 -
Is There A Fourth Reich Already? .... - 126 -

Chapter 3 Exploring The Nazi Connection .... - 127 -
The Ever Changing Ufos .... - 128 -
The Secrets Of The Vril And Thule.. - 128 -
Rudolph Hess And The 'Truth' On Film .... - 129 -
Downloading The Brain Of Rudolph Hess .... - 129 -
Nazis From A Parallel Universe .... - 131 -
The Portal To Mars .... - 131 -

Chapter 4 Over Half A Century On The Moon............................... - 133 -
On The Moon In 1942... - 133 -
One Hand Washes The Other .... - 134 -
Mars Or Bust.. - 136 -
Actual Bases That Come Soon After .... - 138 -
Base Number One .... - 139 -
Base Number Two .... - 140 -
Base Number Three .... - 141 -
Putting Two And Two Together... - 141 -

Chapter 5 Frank Znidarsic's Search For "Free Energy"................ - 143 -
First Things First .... - 143 -
Something From Nothing .... - 144 -
Controlling Gravity .... - 145 -
What Is Cold Fusion? .... - 145 -
Blowing Smoke .... - 148 -
Znidarsic's Theorem .... - 148 -
Where Does This Lead?... - 149 -
Some Helpful Clarification... - 150 -
Znidarsic On Tesla .... - 151 -
More Future Possibilities... - 152 -
The Potential Of The Universe .... - 155 -
Rejected By Mainstream Science .... - 156 -
Too Much Of Nothing .... - 157 -
A Question Of Ridicule .... - 158 -
Manmade Ufos? .... - 159 -
No Good Deed Goes Unpunished .... - 160 -

Chapter 6 The Mysterious Nikola Tesla....................................... - 163 -
Some Of Swartz's Personal History .... - 163 -
The Secret Life Of Nikola Tesla... - 165 -
The Battle With Thomas Edison .... - 166 -
Big Oil In Control .... - 167 -
Tesla And Free Energy.. - 168 -
Continuing Tesla's Work .... - 170 -

Chapter 7 The Mars/Tesla Connection ....- 173 -
   Swartz And Michael X ....- 173 -
   A Puzzling Statement By Dr. Hynek ....- 174 -
   Seances And A Secret Society ....- 175 -
   A Voice From Mars ....- 175 -
   More Mysterious Voices ....- 176 -
   Tesla Joins The Club ....- 177 -
   Fly Me To Mars ....- 178 -
   Tesla's Faulty Tower ....- 179 -
   Was The Mars Mission A Partial Success? ....- 180 -
   Martian Technology, Human Ufos ....- 182 -

Chapter 8 Alternative Three A Scientist Testifies ....- 185 -
   What Is "Alternative Three?" ....- 185 -
   The Moon, Mars And The Zetans ....- 186 -
   Different Mars, Moon Landing Scenarios ....- 187 -
   The Testimony Of One Who's Been There ....- 188 -
   Time Travel "Jumpgates" On The Red Planet ....- 189 -
   The Fascination Continues ....- 190 -

Chapter 9 Communicating With Mars ....- 193 -
   L. G. Lawrence - Communication By Accident.......................- 195 -
   Gregory Hodowanec - Gravitational Signals ....- 196 -

Chapter 10 The Race To Mars...- 205 -
   Secret Experiments ....- 208 -
   The Secret City ....- 209 -
   Al Bielek And The Portal Between Earth And Mars ....- 211 -
   Al Bielek Talks About Mars ....- 212 -

Chapter 11 Antigravity And The New Tesla Physics ....- 217 -
   The Research Of T. Townsend Brown....................................- 218 -
   Tesla Physics In The 21st Century..- 219 -

Early astronomers marveled at what they saw through their telescopes. The weird movements they observed on the surface of the moon and Mars indicated to them that their might be life on these heavenly bodies.

FROM THE EARTH TO THE MOON AND BEYOND – EXPOSING AN INVISIBLE EMPIRE

This may be one of the strangest stories ever told!
At first it seems like a complete fantasy!
A fabrication!
Someone has drunk too much.
The Ayahasca is flowing too freely.

Certainly strange lights and configurations have been seen throughout the ages   on and near the lunar and Martian surfaces, with both the naked eye and all manner of telescopes. There are all sorts of anomalies to account for when we talk about the cosmos and specifically our nearest neighbors in space. But do these celestial bodies, with which we are more familiar than other heavenly bodies, house actual cities and bases? Astronomers – both professional and amateur – have gathered a great deal of evidence that can confirm for us the possibility that someone is UP THERE and in all likelihood LOOKING DOWN upon us and have been doing so for ages.

So what we want to know is: who is responsible for these cosmic shenanigans that have us scratching our head when we look up at the universe and ask what the hell is going on right under our very eyes?

There would, indeed, seem to be bases, ancient cities, all sorts of weird artifacts on the moon and on the Martian surface. But who put them there, and were they left behind recently or are they of ancient vintage? The unexplainable aerial activity all around us would seem to indicate this is an ongoing performance. Someone else is sharing the same space that we are and utilizing all sorts of advanced technologies to fly around directly overhead and plant themselves a million or more miles away.

From the sighting of humongous boomerangs and triangle-shaped objects, it would seem that there is a Secret Space Program going on operated by a consortium or cabal who is heading up a worldwide surveillance program. That someone is flying around with equipment that our government and military denies having access to, although they supposedly have complete control of the sovereign space over our nation.

The evidence as to who is responsible is rather distant, and we can only speculate at this junction.

One would think that extraterrestrials might be the ones responsible for leaving behind evidence of their having camped out in our solar system. We know that no country here on Earth has constructed a Face on Mars, or a bridge across 20 miles of the lunar surface at an altitude of 5 miles. After all, NASA has not done a stellar job of keeping their own minimal space program on track. So it would look like we have to focus our attention elsewhere for those who might be to blame for this irresponsible behavior.

There are some who assert that the Nazi's actually developed a radically different form of space travel and jutted off into space during the final days of WWII to established remote headquarters on the moon and further away on Mars. There is even a movie IRON SKY which espouses this theme, which will be released worldwide in 2012 in a sort of modernized version of 'Dr. Strangelove,' but with an even more whacky theme.

Of course, the former Soviet empire has been accused of every misdeed, so why not of usurping our right to control our own airspace in the case of the mysterious triangles, which seem to be associated with this Invisible Space Program? In all honesty, the Soviets would seem to be down really low on the credibility scale as the villains in our scenario.

Equally as strange is the suspicion that one or more Secret Society is behind this that we officially are told nothing about.

There are those we quote herein who say the Freemasons have known about ET's behavior patterns for a long time since their occult wisdom would include the notion that other entities abound alongside us on an invisible plane even if society refuses to acknowledge their existence. There is proof that numerous American astronauts are high initiates of this mystical order whom some see as having diabolical connections to the dark side. Apparently, these space travelers have even carried with them symbols of the Masonic organization and placed them on the moon (and maybe even on Mars, if they have gotten that far) as a symbol of their divine authority over humankind. Other secret societies, unnamed at this point, may also be responsible for this secondary space program. Nikola Tesla, famed mental wizard, may have shared his knowledge of crossing space and time with a group of inventors as long as a hundred years ago, thus giving them the drop on our own space program. And, if we read matters correctly, they have decided to keep their distance and not let us in on their unincorporated franchise.

One of the more interesting theories is that of a Breakaway Civilization, a shadowy domain that coexists alongside our own world, but keeps to itself in order to either avoid conflict or determine its own destiny. It could be a physical, materialistic civilization or something more fringe, such as a less dense society which exists outside our own dimension in another realm we have no open contact with. . . and they prefer it that way.

The late Ben Rich headed up Lockheed's secret research and development entity

So what we have determined is that their might be 'men' walking around on the moon and/or Mars. But you will have to decide who rules the roost. Who is behind this. Is it 'them' or an undeclared 'us?'

Or perhaps a collaboration of both parties who feel comfortable in going behind the backs of John Q. Citizen and keeping this all so hush-hush as to seem like a dream, or a nightmare of untold proportions.

Before his death, the Father of the Stealth Bomber and Head of the Lockheed Skunk Works shocked everyone when he confessed that the military and the private sector have flying vehicles that mimic alien craft.

The article was written by Tom Keller, an aerospace engineer who has worked as a computer systems analyst for NASA's Jet Propulsion Laboratory. Keller reported that:

1. 'Inside the Skunk Works (Lockheed's secret research and development entity), we were a small, intensely cohesive group consisting of about fifty veteran engineers and designers and a hundred or so expert machinists and shop workers. Our forte was building technologically advanced airplanes of small number and of high class for highly secret missions.'

2. 'We already have the means to travel among the stars, but these technologies are locked up in black projects, and it would take an act of God to ever get them out to benefit humanity. Anything you can imagine, we already know how to do.'

3. 'We now have the technology to take ET home. No, it won't take someone's lifetime to do it. There is an error in the equations. We know what it is. We now have the capability to travel to the stars. First, you have to understand that we will not get to the stars using chemical propulsion. Second, we have to devise a new propulsion technology. What we have to do is find out where Einstein went wrong.'

4. When Rich was asked how UFO propulsion worked, he said, 'Let me ask you. How does ESP work?' The questioner responded with, 'All points in time and space are connected?' Rich then said, 'That's how it works!'

One way or another, the cat is out of the bag. We will shortly meet the culprit or culprits head on and hopefully be able to control our own destiny without the hindrance of some undetermined force – whomever it might be.

MYSTERIOUS TRIANGLES AND A BREAKAWAY CIVILIZATION

Richard Dolan is one of the most respected figures in the UFO community. In a field crowded by overzealous believers and fringe 'contactees,' Dolan has firmly established a reputation as a researcher and author who relies primarily on public and proven sources, or at least sources whose background can be verified in real-world terms. He has written two very influential books on the government cover-up of the UFO phenomenon, 'UFOs and the National Security State,' Volumes One and Two, that provide thorough research into the history of the clandestine, black budget response of the US military and intelligence community to the alien presence.

WHY BELIEVE IN A SECRET SPACE PROGRAM?

Dolan answered that question by saying there are a couple of reasons.

'First,' he said, 'I think that there are a number of anomalous events we know have occurred in Earth orbit and beyond Earth orbit. Those alone are not proof of a secret space program, but I'll go over why I think this is important evidence. We've got 40 years of events recorded by US and Soviet astronauts of objects in orbit that appear to be not our own and that seemed to move intelligently. We've got them going back to the 1960s, and there are some very excellent Soviet cosmonaut reports from the 1980s. We have the evidence of what's known as DSP satellites – that's Defense Support Program satellites. These are a series of geosynchronous satellites in Earth orbit that have a long record of tracking 'fast-walkers' in space. That is, objects that are like a space UFO.

'From the 1973 period up to 1991,' he continued, 'there were, if I'm not mistaken, 281 such anomalous events recorded by the DSP satellites. Now, I'm not saying that every one of these recorded anomalous events are ET craft. But a number of them are really bizarre. For example, one that took place around 1984, recorded by satellite, showed an object that approached it to within a certain very close distance and then moved away. In fact, it approached from a point in deep space and then moved on.'

Astronaut Edgar Mitchel and Richard Dolan. The space traveler says he knows UFOs are real and that one crashed outside of Roswell, NM in 1947.

We have this information, Dolan said, through almost an accident. A friend of Dolan's who worked for many years at an aerospace company received mistakenly, but not illegally, a printout of some DSP 'fast-walker' events.

'My point is simply this: you've got those events and quite a few others that are intriguing, which tells me there is something going on in Earth's orbit that's not being officially explained. It would seem to me very logical that just as there would be a covert monitoring of the UFO phenomenon within Earth's atmosphere and on the ground and so forth, if there are anomalous activities going on in space, then clearly you would want an agency to monitor that as well, to deal with it. And that would necessitate the creation of a very clandestine component to the US space program.'

Secondly, Dolan pointed to the fact that there has also been a good history, although not an 'airtight' history, of leaks from within the military world. One former Air Force NCO (Non-Commissioned Officer) stated that he had the opportunity to review NASA images of the far side of the moon, images that, Dolan said, are normally airbrushed to conceal artificial structures not deemed suitable for release to the public.

'You get the claim quite a few times,' Dolan said, 'of NASA airbrushing and doctoring their moon photographs. Again, these are claims. But I look at a number of these claims and they strike me as sincere individuals and, frankly, I have no reason to doubt what they're saying. There have been at least three or four specific individuals who made these claims about NASA airbrushing their images. So that makes me think that there's more funny business going on. They're hiding something important about space.'

Another of Dolan's sources told Dolan that he had been assigned to train remote viewers at Fort Meade, Maryland, to scan the dark side of the moon, presumably looking for evidence of an alien presence there. Dolan says he feels that the US military must have had a good reason for pursuing that line of investigation and that there are capabilities vis-à-vis space that our military has which they're no telling to the rest of us.

WHAT ABOUT MARS?

'My own thoughts on Mars are this,' Dolan began. 'I have become persuaded over the years that there are things on Mars that seem anomalous to me, that do seem artificial. I will go that far. There are claims by people who are alleged insiders who have gone to Mars and so forth, and I do not credit these claims. Until they're able to prove something that actually sounds rational or is backed by evidence, I can't take it seriously.

'Having said that, though,' he continued, 'look, it makes perfect sense to me, when you look at the history of apparent UFO crashes and recoveries, and there are a number I think there are good cases for, you have to assume that the national security apparatus isn't going to just be sitting on their hands looking at this technology forever. Of course they're going to try to study it and obviously to replicate it. How could they not?'

So that allows 40 to 50 years, according to Dolan, with a lot of black budget money and a lot of secrecy, in which a classified reverse-engineering group could work.

'And if you've had any level of success with it,' Dolan went on, 'it's not something you can share with the world. Yet it would be something that would come in very handy for covert missions beyond Earth's orbit, i.e., a secret space program.'

Dolan says he has spoken to people he considers credible who affirm there is a secret program connected with the moon. Concerning Mars, he says he's never gotten anything that could allow him to say confidently one way or the other, but, he said, he would not be shocked to learn that we had traveled to Mars as a result of recovered alien technology.

'Every conclusion in science,' he added, 'is provisional and contingent on more information coming your way.'

THE BREAKAWAY CIVILIZATION

'One of the ideas I've been kicking around for the last few years,' Dolan said, 'is that of a 'breakaway civilization.' I think that this is something that is real. Now, my theory of it is that it originated really in post-World War II society, but there's nothing preventing such a thing from having happened earlier. The basic idea of the 'breakaway civilization' is simply that you have a secret group, a classified group of people, with access to radically advanced technology, radically advanced science, and they just don't share it with the rest of the world. One scientific breakthrough leads to another, and that leads to another and so on. So the next thing you know, you've got a separate group of humanity that is vastly far beyond the rest of the world.'

Dolan said this isn't necessarily a farfetched notion.

'In our own official world history,' he explained, 'you go back 200 years and compare levels of technology from Europe to, say, Central Africa, and you're talking about two vastly different ways of understanding the world. So really, what is the difficulty in understanding that a classified, secret scientific community would make radical breakthroughs that they wouldn't share? I don't think it's outrageous, and I do think this has happened since World War II. Now, one of the breakthroughs they've made is in what we would call 'antigravity technology.' Now, could this have happened in the 19th century? I don't think that it's impossible in theory.

'I have speculated privately many times,' he said, 'whether there has been a secret breakaway group going back to ancient times. When you look at some of the really puzzling mysteries of our ancient world, whether it's the Great Pyramid of Giza or Macchu Picchu, there are elements of those and other architectural sites that have been left behind that to me at least don't make a whole lot of sense in the context of human society as it then was supposed to have existed. The Great Pyramid doesn't make sense to me in terms of 2,500 years ago ancient Egyptian culture. I wonder if this was a human construct at the time, and what human civilization are we talking about here?

'So I leave open the possibility that some great secret would be understood by a very small, elect group of people. They would want to hide this from the rest of the world for obvious reasons – power, and just not wanting to share.'

THE 'SOPHISTICATED' NAZIS

Asked where the Nazis fit into this picture, Dolan replied, 'When I started getting into this business about 15 years ago, I certainly had a very poor appreciation of just how sophisticated the research was in this field. I've definitely come to a very different opinion now.

'The Nazis were quite sophisticated,' he continued, 'in their science of what we would call 'flying saucer technology.' We now know this. Here's the problem, though, with that theory. I don't think one can state the case that the Nazis explain the entire UFO phenomenon. Not even close.'

Dolan said he had visited the Canadian National Archives in Ottawa to review Canadian UFO reports and came across a story written by an elderly man in the 1980s, who wrote about his experience in the Northwest Territory doing aerial mapping for the Canadian government in 1936. According to Dolan, the man had a perfect, crystal clear sighting of 'the most beautiful aerial object he had ever seen.' The object was oblong, a little longer than it was wide, and he stood looking up, just amazed at what he was seeing. The object took off and within two seconds was at the horizon. It never at any point made a sound.

A typical, even classic UFO sighting, right? But Dolan's point was more about when it occurred.

'It is true,' he said, 'that in 1936 the Nazis were in power. But it's also true that in 1936 their science in this field was still in its bare infancy, as far as anyone could tell. Let's assume that this story is true. That tells me that in 1936 you've got a perfectly functioning, incredible UFO in the middle of nowhere in Northern Canada doing, well, what? What the hell was that thing doing there? Someone's supposed to tell me that's Nazi technology? Sorry, but no sale. I'm not buying that.

'People who argue that UFOs are strictly Nazi technology need to do a little more research into the phenomenon itself. It goes back much further than the 1930s, that's for sure. It's either a very, very clandestine human intelligence that exists as a longstanding secret society – of course we need to find their manufacturing plant and where the hell they're located – or we're dealing with nonhumans here that are interacting with Planet Earth. I actually think the latter theory is more likely, but there certainly is a clandestine human power structure. I don't dispute that.

'But there are just too many witness claims and descriptions of nonhuman entities. I don't believe these are all just faked or screen memories. I think people are actually seeing entities that are not human.'

THE SECRET SPACE PROGRAM

SO WHO IS RUNNING THE SHOW?

'I've tried to figure this one out myself,' Dolan said. 'Who's really running the show here? At least the human part of it. I scratch my head about that frequently. It's certainly not the president of the United States. It's obvious that there is a power structure behind every president. You look at every president of the last almost 50 years and really every one of them got into office because one man named David Rockefeller nodded his head and said, yes, that man's going in.

'That's just how it is. Rockefeller was instrumental behind Gerald Ford. He and Zbigniew Brzezinski practically literally lifted Jimmy Carter up from Georgia and plunked him in the White House. Rockefeller was very powerful and prominent in the Reagan administration. He was essentially the political grandfather of George Herbert Walker Bush. Bush was always a protégé of Kissinger, and Kissinger always worked for Rockefeller. Bill Clinton was very much desired by the Rockefeller people. Clinton attended his first Bilderberger meeting in 1991, the year before he got the Democratic nomination. No accident. And on it goes. Who's one of Obama's senior aides, advisors? It's Brzezinski, the Rockefeller man.

'So all of these presidents are backed, not just by David Rockefeller, who obviously is in his mid- to late-90s now, but that clique of financial power that surrounds him. This is the locus of real power in the world today. My supposition is simply that – just as global financial interests are the dominant force behind US foreign policy and US financial policy – so too I believe they are probably the dominant players in managing UFO technology and the secret space program. I believe that, but I can't prove it.'

The most tangible thing Dolan feels he can point to is that special access programs, the primordial black budget programs, in the US, all indicate a preponderance of private power as opposed to public power.

'In other words,' he explained, 'the US Department of Defense personnel do not appear to be the key players in these special access programs. Rather, it's private contractors, like Boeing or

Lockheed or General Electric and so forth. They really run the show. What we have is, at the classified level, private money that is more likely calling the shots. That's how the government has operated for more than a century, and it makes sense to me that the UFO technology issue would become privatized at some point, and the secret, clandestine space program would also be to a large extent privatized. It certainly would help with secrecy. It's easier to have something proprietary instead of merely classified, if you want to keep a secret, and I think a lot of this has gone into private hands.'

While government institutions may still have 'their fingers in the pie,' Dolan said, the technology and knowledge that's truly important is outside the public realm and it's outside the public purview.

DOMINATING SPACE

Is NASA part of the cover-up?

'My feeling has been,' Dolan answered, 'that NASA is a front for something that's much more profound behind the scenes. Think of it this way: the United States is never, ever going to relinquish its dominance of space as a platform of operations. After all, it is the domination of space that enables the US military to dominate theaters of war. Without dominating space, the US military honestly isn't any better than the military of a lot of other nations. But because we dominate space with satellite technology, that is how we allow Stealth fighters and bombers to get the exact information they need that enables them to do precision targeting and bombing and so forth. The militarization of space is an absolute necessity from a national security perspective. There is nothing in the world that will ever make them voluntarily relinquish that.'

In recent years, however, NASA has ended manned space missions and has announced a much more stripped down future agenda.

'That's going to be a completely separate development from the clandestine military component of space,' Dolan said. 'So, on that basis alone, I think it's an obvious given that we have a secret space program. That doesn't have to include a connection to the UFO/ET phenomenon. But I think it does simply because I'm quite satisfied that there IS a UFO/ET phenomenon and that some of it exists in Earth orbit.'

WHO IN GOVERNMENT KNOWS ABOUT ALL THIS?

'You mean our elected officials?' Dolan asked. 'Members of Congress, if any of them know anything about this, then we're not talking about any more than a handful. Maybe three or four, tops, probably have any legitimate information on this. Guaranteed, it wouldn't be more than that. Presidents? I once spoke to a senior retired CIA officer, a very high-level man, who knows on a first name basis something like five or six former Directors of Central Intelligence. He's a very well-connected man.

'He's someone also relatively famous and unfortunately I can't tell you who he is. But I asked him on one occasion, how much do US presidents know? A simple question. I think everyone wants to know that. His answer was, well, some have known more than others. He made it clear to me that Jimmy Carter was briefed. He made it clear to me that he's 99 percent sure that Ronald Reagan was briefed. He was very confident but not 100 percent certain that George Herbert Walker Bush was briefed thoroughly on this. After that, he said, it gets a little more muddy. It was his opinion that from Clinton onward it's less of a sure thing that these presidents have been briefed thoroughly.'

The CIA-connected source said that presidents come and go, but the bureaucrats who run the secret space program stay. And presidents are not always reliable. Some are very dedicated, others are a little more distracted. He didn't have a lot of confidence in the abilities of the presidency as an institution to manage this problem.

'What do presidents really do?' Dolan said. 'They've got to kiss babies; they've got to meet and greet dignitaries. They've got all these political issues they have to deal with. The president is basically a spokesperson for the government. It's very difficult for a president to be on top of the whole mass of covert operations going on within the intelligence community. He can't be. It's just not possible physically, logistically. And for a president to be aware of this particular problem? No. Sometimes it's better off that he not be aware of it, so he can do his job in the other realms of government.'

RESPONDING TO THE ALIEN PRESENCE

Given that a secret space program exists, what would be its ultimate goal?

'My feeling,' Dolan replied, 'would be that it's a separate thing altogether from basic neo-geopolitical maneuvering. What you would use a secret space program for is to deal with these 'others,' as I call them, these other beings, one way or another.'

Dolan offered the following story to make his point about keeping certain technology secret: 'Back in 1986, when the United States bombed the nation of Libya, is very instructive. Because at that time, the US had operationally, but still secret, the F-117-A Nighthawk Stealth Fighter. Yet the Stealth Fighter was not employed in that Libyan mission. Instead, the US used the F-111. Now, the F-111 is a very fine aircraft, but the fact was that the top of the line fire aircraft was the Stealth fighter, and it wasn't used on the Libyan mission. The question is, why not?

'The answer, we learn from the military, was simply that the F-117 classification was still secret, and the Libyan mission was not seen as a high enough priority to risk exposing that aircraft yet. The US did not want the rest of the world to know because Stealth technology was just that important. And that should tell us something: that just because you have top of the line technology out there, using it in such a way that it's out in the open is not always a good thing. The technology can be so valuable that it's almost counterproductive to use it because then you're letting the rest of the world know you've got it.

'So too with secret space technology and the secret space program. Using flying saucers to fight the wars in Afghanistan and Iraq would be counterproductive from their point of view. That's assuming that they want to win the wars to begin with. But once you use them in battle, you're alerting other groups that yes, this is possible and you can build a functioning flying saucer. And maybe the US doesn't want them to know that.'

Dolan continued by saying that the capabilities of such technology would obviously be used for the highest level of classified activity that exists, and in his view that's the ET reality.

'This technology would primarily be used for that,' he said, adding, 'in all its nebulous glory. I don't know all of the interactions that the terrestrial power structure might have with these 'others.' But I can imagine that there may have been interactions and that this technology would be considered very important in that regard.'

WOULD THAT INCLUDE TRIANGLE SHIPS?

'Well, I've been looking at triangles for a while myself,' Dolan said. 'There's definitely a proliferation of triangles sightings – that is, the perfect triangle craft. And of course, as you know, there aren't supposed to be any. In the inventories of all the militaries of the world, there are no openly acknowledged, perfect triangular craft, not one. Now, we've got rumors of things like the TR-3, the Black Manta. There are a lot of sightings of triangles near the Boeing plant in Seattle. There have been a number of these recorded.

'I believe that we are making some of these triangles,' he continued. 'There's a crystal clear sighting of a perfect triangle craft from 1989 over the North Sea by one of the most experienced aviation experts in the world at that time. A guy named Chris Gibson, who used to compete in aircraft recognition contests. They'd flash an image of an aircraft at you for a couple of seconds and you'd have to identify it. This guy saw a perfect triangle in a refueling operation with a KC-135 and couple of F-111s accompanying it. And the guy's adamant. A witness like that is someone it's very tough to refute. So I think we've been building triangles for a while.'

Dolan adds a cautionary note, saying that it is also true that in some encounters with triangles, there appeared to be some of the same 'high strangeness' as with more recognizably alien craft. Things like time distortions and apparent abduction experiences with nonhumans are also part of the triangle mystery.

'We are probably building some triangles,' Dolan said, 'but I would stop short of saying that we are building ALL of the triangles.'

THE CASH-LANDRUM INCIDENT

The Cash-Landrum incident remains a famous case of a debilitating UFO encounter. In Texas in December 1980, two women traveling in their car saw an unusual craft in the sky accompanied by several black, apparently military helicopters. The women sued the government unsuccessfully for funds to cover their medical expenses after they received radiation burns and suffered other medical complications in the wake of their sighting.

'I think most of the good money on that case,' Dolan said, 'is that that is a US experimental craft. It's certainly the case that you've got an object accompanied by lots of helicopters. So it appears to be something that's ours. It appeared to be in some kind of operational trouble. It was highly radioactive, which also makes it more likely that it might have been ours.'

Dolan acknowledged that other UFO investigators he considered credible, such as John Schuessler, always believed that the object was not manufactured by the US.

'But John could be wrong,' Dolan said. 'He's a very good investigator and a good man, but, I don't know, my inclination is to think that that object was one of our own.'

WHAT WE KNOW AND WHAT WE DON'T KNOW

When asked if he had any concluding remarks, Dolan spoke about the need for proof in a field where so much must be taken on faith.

'We're in a field,' he said, 'where there are certain things we know and there are certain things we don't know. And we always have to remember the difference.

'One thing that I can say we know,' he continued, 'is that there is a genuine UFO phenomenon and that this phenomenon has engaged with the United States military for many years. We KNOW this is true because we have a certain number of released US documents that prove it. That prove we have been concerned about UFOs; that we have tried to intercept UFOs; and we have seen them – military personnel – visually and tracked them on radar. All of that and more. That is unarguable and you can take it to the bank.

'Much of the rest is guesswork. And it's fair to guess. We have to guess. We have to create hypotheses. The only thing that I try to remind myself and others of is that when we're creating a hypothesis, we need to distinguish that from known fact. We've got to be careful how we handle our evidence. I speculate as much as anyone at this point in the game. I'm very happy to speculate. I just want to make it clear to people who read what I have to say that or listen to me, that when I come to a conclusion, A, it's always a provisional conclusion, and B, it's always based on what I consider to be evidence.'

Dolan said he wasn't totally happy to use secret, inside sources in his work because it put people in the position of having to choose whether to trust him or not based on the claims of a source he could not bring before the public. It's much better to work efficiently from public, certified sources and carefully assemble one's hypothesis on that basis.

'We're in deep waters,' Dolan said. 'It's very easy to lose our footing. It's very easy to drown. You've got to be careful.'

And so we leave behind Mr. Richard Dolan, a most reasonable and responsible individual who is as eager as we all are to find out who maintains this secret space program we have grown so accustomed to hearing about, and just how far ahead of the curve they are likely to be.

Get ready now to venture forth into uncharted waters. Our journey may not be easy at times. There are likely to be those who will attempt to block our way. But we are bright and intelligent and want to know the answers, so we will persevere in our effort to get to the bottom of the mystery at hand.

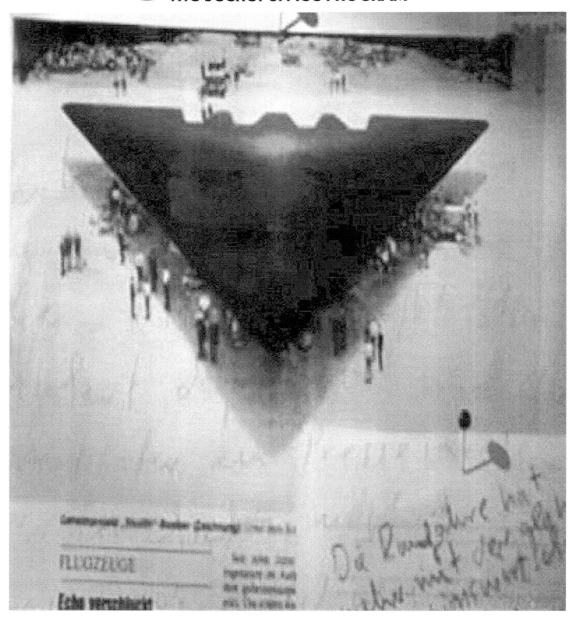

"There's definitely a proliferation of triangles sightings – that is, the perfect triangle craft," or so says Richard Dolan, who notes that sightings of a hypothetical craft known as the Black Manta has been observed repeatedly near the Seattle Boeing Plant. Is this a legitimate picture of one such "faster than a speeding bullet" aircraft?

THE MARTIAN EYE IN THE SKY HAS ALWAYS BEEN LOOKING DOWN ON US!

The planet Mars certainly has played an important part in the age of flying saucers.

Many of the early UFO contactees claimed that they had established a variety of friendships – close cosmic bonds – with visitors from the Red Planet. They even wrote books which maintained that they traveled into space and visited the nearby planets. UFO fixtures George Adamski and Howard Menger both say they flew off to Mars and were returned safely. One country boy from Arkansas who used to wear overalls when he spoke publicly even says he made friends with a big old shaggy Martian dog by the name of Bo. Hardly anyone believed Buck Nelson, but he was a likable enough guy so no one begrudged him his stories.

Some of the book titles of the genre include 'Flying Saucer From Mars' by Cedric Allingham,' and 'My Trip To Mars, the Moon and Venus,' by Buck Nelson, which is not to neglect numerous Martian-driven comics and chewing gum-inspired 'Invaders From Mars' trading cards.

The notion of 'Men From Mars' has been burning in our souls since time immemorial, but more specifically has been with us in spades for well over a century now, due to writers like Edgar Rice Burroughs and H.G. Wells, who took us where no man had gone before. We also saw Hollywood explode with movies like 'Mars Attacks' and 'War of the Worlds,' and, more recently, 'Independence Day,' but there is much more to the history of early beliefs about life on Mars.

A website called 'War of the Worlds: The Historical Perspective,' does its best to give us an overview of the many phases our beliefs about Mars have gone through.

'The Babylonians were the first to record the existence of Mars,' the posting reads, 'in approximately 400 BC, calling it Nergal. Nergal was the underworld personification of the sun god Utu and the god of the netherworld, bringing war, pestilence, fever and devastation. The Romans, like the Babylonians, imbued the planet with the nature of violence and death. To the Romans, the planet was Aries or Mars, the God of War. He was generally portrayed as in full battle attire with a crested helmet and shield.'

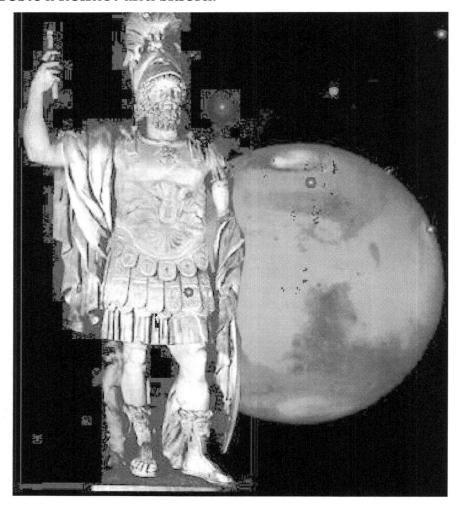

The Romans imbued the red planet with the nature of violence and death. To the Romans, the planet was Aries or Mars, the God of War. He was generally portrayed as in full battle attire with a crested helmet and shield.

The modern age of observation of Mars began in the 1500s, when the Danish astronomer Tycho Brahe made some excellent observations of the planet that were sufficiently accurate for his student, Johannes Kepler, to prove in 1609 that the orbit of Mars was elliptical rather than circular. One might note that Brahe was a unique character. Having lost a portion of his nose in a duel, he replaced it with a prosthetic one made of gold and silver.

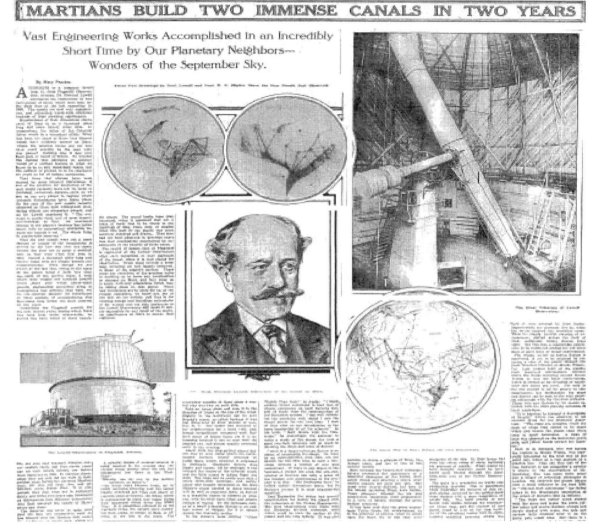

It is doubtful they would report such a discovery today, but a 1911 edition of the NY Times describes how the Martians have spent two years building another canal.

Galileo Galilei was also studying Mars in 1609, the first time it was seen through a telescope, ushering in a new age of detailed observation. Some years later, an astronomer named Christiaan Huygens drew the first map of Mars. He was also the first to speculate, in 1698, about the existence of life on Mars. This led to the further popularization of the idea by Sir William Herschel, the discoverer of the planet Uranus. He concluded that, in spite of the thin atmosphere on Mars, the Martians 'probably enjoy a situation similar to our own.' He also interpreted the dark areas on Mars as seas and light areas as land.

'Many other astronomers would continue to postulate the existence of life on the planet,' the report continues. 'Angelo Secchi observed Mars in 1858 and describes features he called 'canali.' The idea of canals stuck. But more than any other person, it was to be astronomer Percival Lowell who would do the most to advance the cause of the canals and life on Mars.'

Lowell began his observations at Flagstaff, Arizona, in 1894, and the following year published the first of three sensational books in which he argued that the so-called canals represented the work of a Martian civilization and were in fact a vast irrigation system. He declared that the lines of the canals were too precisely and intelligently organized and constructed to be a matter of mere chance.

'Of course it was just a few years later,' the posting says, 'in 1897, that H. G. Wells would publish his 'War of the Worlds,' in which a race of Martians are losing the fight to irrigate their dying world.' Around the world many hundreds of editions of this science fiction classic have been published in probably just about every language. On the silver screen there have been several cinematic renderings, the last major one starring Hollywood superstar Tom Cruise.

During the spiritualism craze of the late 1800s, mediums were not only likely to be contacting your Uncle Ernie, but were just as typically speaking in the tongue of a Martian. As a primary example, there is the case of Catherine Elise Muller of Geneva, who visited Mars while in a stone cold trace state via astral travel where she described all manner of life forms, from the most highly advanced inhabitants down to the lowest orders of animal and plant life.

A LITTLE LATER ON

In the 20th century would come the many space probes sent to Mars, first by the Soviet Union. The first successful probe was America's 1965 effort, Mariner 4, which managed to fly by the Red

Planet and send back 22 images of the surface. Both the US's Mars Pathfinder, which landed on Mars in 1997, and the European probe called Mars Express, continue to send back quality images of Mars. More probes are planned, but a manned mission to Mars is still needed to answer many of the continuing mysteries.

'For now, that is just a dream of the mission planners,' the report says, 'but the possibility of life existing even now on Mars at a microbiological level is a great enticement to send human explorers. And who knows, they might yet also find evidence that Mars was once home to higher forms of life.'

Our exploration of Mars seems impressive at this point, but it is also true that we have examined only a small part of the surface of the planet. Mars continues to hide many mysteries, and the existence of biological life there is but one of them.

Then there is the ever-popular theory that life on Mars is invisible to the human eye because the indigenous race there vibrates at a higher rate than we can see. Did this higher race have some need for the canals and the pyramids and even cities some believe to exist to the surface? If so, why have they deserted them? Something to ponder as we soldier on in our quest for the truth.

IS THERE A SECRET ET PRESENCE ON THE MOON AND MARS?

Our research abounds with material on the secret space program and the ET-related conspiracy theories that accompany it. There are numerous blogs and sites on the Internet to digest and so it takes considerable time to decipher every one of them before you can decide for yourself where some of these claims rate on your personal 'truth meter.'

In a long posting called 'UFOs and Reported Extraterrestrials On Mars,' writer Steve Omar opens by saying, 'Apollo moon astronauts were often followed to the moon, at times, by UFOs. Official NASA Apollo 12 photograph AS12-497319 clearly shows a large UFO hovering over an astronaut walking on the moon.'

Omar also lists the supposedly magnanimous claims of Christopher Kraft, the director of the NASA tracking base in Houston during the Apollo moon missions. Sometime after leaving his NASA job, he is quoted as having revealed that the following conversation had taken place (the astronauts' responses are labeled in the plural, not by individual name):

Astronauts Neil Armstrong and Buzz Aldrin speaking from the moon: 'Those are giant things. No, no, no, this is not an optical illusion. No one is going to believe this!'

Mission Control (Houston Center): 'What, what, what? What the hell is happening? What's wrong with you?'

Astronauts: 'They're here under the surface.'

Mission Control: 'What's there? Emission interrupted. Interference control calling Apollo 11.'

Astronauts: 'We saw some visitors. They were here for a while, observing the instruments.'

Mission Control: 'Repeat your last information.'

Astronauts: 'I say that there were other spaceships. They're lined up on the other side of the crater.'

Mission Control: 'Repeat. Repeat.'

Astronauts: 'Let us sound this orbital . . . In 625 to 5 . . . automatic relay connected. My hands are shaking so badly I can't do anything. Film it? God, if these damned cameras have picked up anything . . . what then?'

Mission Control: 'Have you picked up anything?'

Astronauts: 'I don't have any film at hand. Three shots of the saucers or whatever they were that were ruining the film.'

Mission Control: 'Control, control here. Are you on your way? Is the uproar with the UFOs over?'

Astronauts: 'They've landed there. There they are, and they are watching us.'

Mission Control: 'The mirrors, the mirrors . . . have you set them up?'

Astronauts: 'Yes, they're in the right place. But whoever made those spaceships can surely come tomorrow and remove them. Over and out.'

TOO CONTRIVED?

Naturally, we have no proof that these transcriptions are bona fide. In fact, it's hard to accept that the astronauts would use such course language because in real life they go overboard to be such goodie-goodie two shoes. Nor would anyone, especially our spacemen, end a live conversation by using the phrase 'Over and out.'

A gigantic monolith stands tall for all to see on the moon.

But the tense exchange between the astronauts and Mission Control does seem to bear out one recurring theme of the secret space program mythos, that UFOs have been photographed in the vicinity of US astronauts on the moon and those images airbrushed to hide the fact that the extraterrestrials are closely monitoring humankind's space programs. The moon may even be a home base for an alien civilization dating back to before humankind's recorded history.

Omar gives some background on the interest in life on the moon, saying it first grabbed public attention when Nikola Tesla publicly reported his experiences in transmitting radio signals to the moon and attempting to receive answers, which he said had actually happened. Later, American, British and French astronomers reported moving and sometimes even blinking lights during the 1920s and 30s. Their findings were reported in newspapers and even official scientific journals. In the early 1950s, an award-winning astronomer named John O'Neill claimed to have observed a twelve-mile long 'bridge' on the moon that appeared to be artificially and intelligently constructed. The bridge sighting was replicated by other witnesses before the structure was dismantled for unknown reasons.

The list of astronauts who admitted they saw UFOs includes Gordon Cooper (while on Earth) and James McDivitt, who also took UFO photos while orbiting Earth, according to Omar. When the government tracked the flight of UFOs on radar, they often followed the course of the alien ships to the moon. Meanwhile, civilian astronomers continued to record moving, flashing and stationary lights on the moon while US and Soviet astronauts repeatedly photographed mysterious structures there.

Hidden deep in one of the craters of the moon appears to be an unmistakable domed base or city of some sort.

There exist photos of strange spires on the moon that have been found to form perfect geometric patterns. Tall white spires that resemble the Washington Monument were photographed on the lunar surface, along with mysterious straight roads or tracks that cut through craters, hills, valleys and rock piles without a twist. Some of the domes had flashing lights, while several NASA photos showed long, cigar-shaped objects parked on the moon, which later departed in subsequent photos.

Even stranger is an unconfirmed report that when Apollo 11 astronaut Buzz Aldrin opened the door of his craft after landing on the moon, he immediately saw a transparent etheric being staring at him outside.

Omar says that the dark side of the moon, hidden from our eyes and telescopes on Earth, would be a logical place for an ET presence to hide its spaceports, and that perhaps one of the occupants had come to greet Armstrong and Aldrin on the sunny side of the street. Omar then poses the question, 'Could it be that the moon is a foreign country and someone else's property? That the moon government does not want us coming up and invading their territory with our nuclear weapons, pollution, unwelcome military facilities, diseases, litter, mining exploitation and historically proven record of foreign imperialism?'

That may serve as one explanation for NASA's decision to stop sending astronauts to the moon in 1973. The Apollo moon program had been a rousing success and had generated a lot of positive publicity for NASA and been a prestigious achievement for the nation as a whole. But maybe we were preceded there by an alien society who simply didn't want to share the moon with us because they knew we were too screwed up to be good neighbors.

CIVILIZATIONS ON MARS

Omar tells the following story in regard to a Martian civilization:

'In 1959,' he writes, 'a Martian flying disc spacecraft reportedly landed in the wilderness outside of Moscow, in the Soviet Union, where a secret meeting with Soviet Premier Nikita Khrushchev was arranged. The conference regarded improving relations with Earth, exchanging knowledge, and securing world and interplanetary peace, yet the Soviet government rejected the terms.'

The report originated from a former Army Intelligence sergeant who investigated UFOs while in the Army in the 1950s.

Is this a giant crashed spaceship photographed on the lunar surface?

Another story took place on April 24, 1964, when an oval-shaped metallic flying craft landed in a farm field in Newark Valley in New York. Farmer Gary Wilcox drove his tractor to the object, which was clearly visible on a sunny day. He kicked it to make sure it was real, after which two occupants about four feet tall emerged carrying a square tray full of different vegetables they had collected from his farm. When Wilcox confronted them about stealing his crops, they said, 'Don't be alarmed. We have spoken to people before.' Their voices were strange, and they were wearing white, metallic-looking overalls without seams, stitching or pockets. He could not see their hands or feet or see any facial features beneath their space suits.

One of the interlopers stated, 'We are from what you know as the planet Mars. We can only come to Earth every two years.' They also issued a warning that Earth people should stay out of space. The beings spoke in a monotone and rejected his request to travel with them.

Wilcox said he gave them a bag of fertilizer and exchanged information about it and other subjects before the beings entered the craft and took off. His story was later investigated by the local sheriff and he was subjected to a psychiatric examination. In both cases, he was found to be a normal, truthful person with no emotional problems.

If this incident is true – and it has always been a favorite of author/publisher Beckley – it certainly offers at least a working confirmation that there is life on Mars, although perhaps that life would almost assuredly have to survive in the interior of the planet instead of on the harsh Martian surface. But is this all conjecture or what?

After all no one has landed on the Martian or the dark side lunar surfaces to say for sure.

Or have they?

A battle with conventional thinking continues to unfold.

What appears to some researchers to be humanoids, birds, and animals have all seemingly been photographed on the Martian surface.

DID NIKITA KHRUSHCHEV TRY TO SET UP SHOP ON THE MOON?

Living through the Cold War was a frustrating and sometimes frightening experience as you never knew when you might see a mushroom cloud filling the sky off in the distance and a shock wave that would literally blow your socks off your very feet. On one hand Nikita Khrushchev was a funny little man who pounded his shoe on the table at the United Nations, on the other he had his finger on the button that could send us all into oblivion in a matter of seconds.

It is a period one can hardly forget, and it was also a period that saw flying saucers zipping about all over the world, including in the former Soviet Union.

Indeed, both America and Russia had their eyes on the sky and their heads in the clouds with thoughts of space travel and getting to the moon for purposes of earthly domination.

There was indeed a space race of supreme order and we thought it was our patriotic duty to set foot on the lunar surface first and before the Russkies got there. And, in order to do so, we might well have had to turn to one of their Communist allies to do so.

It's a little known 'fact' that the Yugoslavian government had solidified their own secret space program as early as 1950 or thereabouts. In fact, according to a YouTube video called 'Houston, We Have A Problem' that has been downloaded nearly a half of a million times, the Yugoslavian program was the most advanced in the world and had its own astronaut team and its own rockets ready to launch toward the moon. On the Internet you can see the underground facilities in which all of their rocketry was being hidden, along with a complete space city just like the ones the Russians were hoping to construct on the moon itself.

On the Kevin Smith Show, the producer of the forthcoming documentary says that Yugoslavia's benign dictator, Marshall Tito, actually sold the rights to his country's space program to the United States for over a billion dollars during the time of the Kennedy administration, allowing us to get to the moon and back safely.

The Soviet bloc nation of Yugoslavia had its own space program complete with an astronaut program in the 1950s It has been claimed they sold America the information that made it possible for us to beat the Russians to the moon.

It's a strange story and one that needs to be sorted out. But we do know that both the US and the USSR's military were troubled over not only the sightings of UFOs over their respective nations, but the landing of such craft on unsecured soil. Even the mayor of a town in Germany told of seeing a craft on the ground as he traveled across the Soviet Union by train.

With a UFO wave of epidemic proportions, it is no wonder the Soviet Union wanted to set up shop on the moon, where perhaps they could meet the extraterrestrials safely tucked away from the manipulating hands of their Cold War enemies.

When doing some follow-up research for this updated book, we ran across an interesting oddity: a report from the decidedly mainstream publication, 'Science Digest,' their February 1958 issue to be precise, which considered whether the Soviets might have already leaped ahead of the US space program.

The author, Albert Perry, begins by saying, 'We advertise our failures, but the Soviets don't. For all we know, Moscow's scientists and engineers did try to shoot a rocket to the moon last November 7, to celebrate the 40th anniversary of the Communist seizure of Russia, but failed. You will recall that for a while, during that weekend, some mysterious radio signals were heard from outer space. They were not accountable by the two Sputniks, and soon they faded out. We may surmise that, in their try for the moon, the Soviet shooting team took a wrong aim, and that the rocket they fired is now either orbiting around the sun or is lost in space.

'But whether or not there indeed was such an attempt, the Soviets are certain to try sending a rocket to the moon, and soon, too. The moon is very much the Reds' next target. Moscow has laid its plans, and will surely make an effort to carry them out. At first, it will be an unmanned rocket; in fact, several of them. Later, the Soviet rockets to the moon will be manned. Finally, Soviet men will stay on the moon, either for definite periods of time or permanently. Such is the Kremlin's announced agenda.'

Perry goes on to write that Russia had already announced that they will build special lunar cities with unique atmospheric pressures so arranged as to enable humans to survive and thrive on the moon. The Red city will be constructed in one of the lunar craters, under a tremendous dome of glass and furnished with aluminum doors called 'air-locks.' Inside, every half-mile or so, the city will be partitioned by glass walls with double doors. These will minimize the damage that may result from falling meteorites or other accidents. The walls will play a similar role to that now served by an ocean liner's water-tight compartments.

The Russians will also create self-sufficiency on the moon in terms of food, saying that transporting even a mere loaf of bread from the Earth to the moon would cost far too much over the long haul. Because of the difference in gravity, all plants would grow to fantastically large sizes.

'A radish will be as tall as a date palm grows on Earth,' according to Professor N.A. Varvarov, a Russian scientist quoted by Perry. 'Onions will send forth sprouts 33-feet long.'

Perry continues by saying that 'a number of solar and atomic energy stations will be built on the moon by the Soviet man of the future. With the aid of these, the moon's light, water and other necessities will be provided. Aluminum, glass, plastics, oxygen and nitrogen will all come from lunar ores. Soviet men, exploring the moon, exploiting its natural resources, and building those lunar cities, are shown in the recently completed Soviet film, 'Road Into Interstellar Space.' This movie was produced with the help of a large group of Soviet scientists specializing in astrophysics and astronautics.'

The main industry of the future Red lunar settlements will be the manufacture of spaceships and spaceship fuel. For after the moon,

Mars and Venus will be the Soviet targets, with the moon serving as a way station and a ship-and-fuel depot en route to those planets.

Perry's article goes on to deal with other components of the Soviet space effort, such as then current thinking on multistage rockets for trips to the moon and nearby planets, as well as the belief that Soviet propaganda efforts would be enhanced by their ability to broadcast television programs from space to the entire Earth, not simply

The space race was on and the Russians took it very seriously.

Russia itself, which is of course a precursor of communication and broadcast satellites so familiar to our own era.

'Will the Soviets have a legal title to the moon, and later to other heavenly bodies,' Perry asks, 'if they are the first to reach those outer worlds?'

Landing alone is not enough, says Dr. Norman McKenzie, one of Canada's leading experts in international law. 'Possession and Control' constitute the only formula, he states, under which any nation on Earth can claim anything above us.

'But that is precisely Moscow's plan,' Perry declares, 'to possess and control anything the Reds reach in outer space. That is why they intend, as soon as they are able, to have human beings in those Soviet interplanetary rockets and to establish permanent man-staffed Russian stations on the moon and further yet.'

The Russians counter such fears, however, by reassuring the US that 'The aim of the Soviet scientists is not at all to build military bases on the moon so as to threaten the United States from there. Our efforts in astronautics are to penetrate the secrets of cosmic space the soonest, to comprehend the measureless universe the deepest.'

One Russian scientist said further that those sorts of fears are 'an absurdity to any sober-thinking military expert in any country, who surely knows that the hoisting of any national flag on the moon should not be the basic goal of any astronauts, be they Soviet or American. The Russian scientist joins a chorus of voices saying that America should be partner in the joint exploration of space, along with scientists from throughout the world.

'And, if we may be a wee bit cynical,' Perry concludes, 'why not? From the Soviet viewpoint, that is, why not? In all such contacts amid our contests, the Soviets would always learn more from our scientists than the Soviets would in their turn impart. At least, they would try to take as much as they could but give little, if anything at all.'

Apart from Perry's obvious Cold War paranoia, certainly typical of the 1950s in the US, is there perhaps a deeper threat to his view of the Soviets' inroads into outer space? What if the machinery and know-how for the Russian cities on the moon were already in place at that point? What if they had already beaten us there and were toying with us by saying it would all be deferred to some future date?

There have always been those who believe that America had a secret space program, but what if the Russians had one as well? Drawing from the same sources, such as suppressed Tesla technology or the alien-driven technology reverse-engineered from crashed flying saucers? Perhaps the Russians weren't merely dreaming big. Perhaps they had already settled on the moon and were waiting to see if we could catch up to them.

SPACE BASES – YOU CAN BLAME THEM ON HITLER!

There is a wide body of science fiction literature, conspiracy theory and stories and claims circulating linking UFOs to Nazi Germany. These theories describe supposedly successful attempts to develop an advanced aircraft or spacecraft prior to and during World War II, and further claim that these craft survived into the postwar world in secret underground bases in Antarctica, South America and the United States, along with their creators.

In effect, there is a sort of a flying saucer mythos that has grown up that encompasses Hitler, the Nazis, a belief in a hollow earth and German-staffed bases at the Poles and on the dark side of the moon.

THE STORY OF IRON SKY

'Towards the end of World War II, the Nazi scientists made a significant breakthrough in anti-gravity. From a secret base built in the Antarctic, the first Nazi spaceships were launched in late '45 to found the military base Schwarze Sonne (Black Sun) on the dark side of the Moon. This base was designed to build a powerful invasion fleet and return to take over the Earth once the time was right.

'Now its 2018, and it's the time for the first American Moon landing since the 70s. Meanwhile the Nazi invasion, that has been over 70 years in the making, is on its way, and the world is goose-stepping towards its doom.'

The above is a 'propaganda quote' from a media kit for a film that has just completed production in the land where the sun seldom shines. A much hyped Sci Fi thriller produced entirely with private funding, this huge looking cinema epic from Finland, IRON SKY, could well be the 'Dr. Strangelove' for the current generation.

Rife with special effects that depict the Nazi flying saucer program, this epic will do its share to provoke controversy over the notion that WWII German scientists put humankind on the moon much earlier than it has been generally believed.

There are some points where German UFO literature conforms largely to documented history. For example, it is true that the German Third Reich claimed the territory of New Swabia in Antarctica, sent an expedition there in 1938, and planned others. It is also true that the German Third Reich conducted research into advanced propulsion technology, including rocketry. A scientist named Viktor Schauberger did a great deal of research into developing flying winged craft and circular winged aircraft. In addition, some UFO sightings during World War II, particularly those known as 'foo fighters,' were thought by the allies to be prototype enemy aircraft designed to harass Allied aircraft through electromagnetic disruption, a technology similar to today's electromagnetic pulse (EMP) weapons.

A dramatic look at a Nazi flying disc in a hangar on the moon courtesy of the producers of "Iron Sky," the movie.

THE STUFF OF LEGENDS

From there, the story grows stranger. In 1950, a former minister of the National Economy under the Mussolini regime named Professor Giuseppe Belluzzo claimed in a newspaper article that 'types of flying discs were designed and studied in Germany and Italy as early as 1942.' Belluzo also said that 'some great power is launching discs to study them.'

The Bell UFO was among the first flying objects to be connected with the Nazis. It apparently had occult markings on it and was said to be similar to a vertical takeoff craft described in a Wehrmacht document. One should note that a bell-shaped UFO crashed in Kecksburg, Pennsylvania, on December 9, 1965. The same month, a German engineer named Rudolph Schriever gave an interview to a German newsmagazine in which he claimed that he had designed a craft powered by a circular plane of rotating turbine blades. He said he had worked on the project with his team at BMW's Prague works until April, 1945, when he fled Czechoslovakia. His designs were later stolen from his workshop in Bremerhaven-Lehe in 1948, and he was convinced that Czech agents had built his craft for 'a foreign power.'

German engineer Georg Klein claimed in 1953 that the Third Reich had developed two types of flying discs. First, a non-rotating disc that was developed at Breslau by V-2 rocket engineer Richard Miethe, which was captured by the Soviets. Klein also spoke of a disc developed by Rudolph Schriever and others at Prague, which consisted of a ring of moving turbine blades around a fixed cockpit. Klein claimed to have witnessed this craft's first manned flight in February of 1945, when it managed to climb to 40,000 feet in three minutes, and attained a speed of 1,400 mph in level flight.

Aeronautical engineer Roy Fedden would later comment that the only craft that could approach the capabilities attributed to flying saucers were those being designed by the Germans toward the end of the war. Fedden had earlier stated that, 'I have seen enough of their designs and production plans to realize that if the Germans had managed to prolong the war some months longer, we would have been confronted with a set of entirely new and deadly developments in air warfare.'

A similar comment was made in 1959 by Captain Edward Ruppelt, the editor of the US Air Force's Project Blue Book. 'When WWII ended,' he said, 'the Germans had several radical types of aircraft and guided missiles under development. The majority were in the most preliminary stages, but they were the only known craft that could even approach the performance of objects reported by UFO observers.'

THE ACCUSATIONS FLY

Beyond the hard science and history related to the alleged German UFOs, what was the real driving force behind Hitler's push to create new aeronautical wonders? In an online posting called 'The Nazi-UFO Connection,' the unnamed writer says, 'Following the war, there is more than enough evidence to conclude that American corporate fascists secreted literally thousands of hardcore Nazis into the USA, shuffling them into the various levels of the military-industrial-intelligence fraternity. In recent years, men like Vladimir Terziski have exposed a literal 'vast right wing conspiracy' involving fascist military-industrial fraternities in Germany, the United States AND in Antarctica, of all places . . . from where hardcore fascists who still believe that Adolph Hitler was a god continue to advance the dark technology which began in the underground bases and concentration camps of World War II Germany.

'S.S. 'pure bred' scientists within the alleged Nazi base in Antarctica, code-named the 'New Berlin,' have been carrying out, in addition to mind control and biogenetic experimentation, continuous research and development in the field of Antigravity propulsion, at least to a ten-fold degree over and beyond the research efforts that were carried out by Nazi scientists during World War II.'

The writer goes on to point out that the American moon program was basically founded on the research of one Nazi 'rocket scientist' named Werner Von Braun, and that rocket propulsion and antigravity propulsion were both an integral part of the Nazi space projects. The writer even asks, 'Could the Nazis have gone to the moon prior to the

USA? There are even reports of Nazi space bases on the moon, and also of massive Nazi bases under the mountains of Neu Schwabenland, Antarctica. And these reports just keep coming.'

HITLER UNDER THE INFLUENCE

'It is a known fact,' the writer continues, 'that Adolph Hitler read a book by Rosicrucian Grandmaster E. Bulwer Lytton, titled 'The Coming Race,' about a subterranean race which possessed supernatural technology and who, according to the novel, were intent on one day claiming the surface world for their own. Probably due to his fascination for occult legendary and mystic tales – such as the Buddhist's traditions of a vast underground world called Agharti and the Hindu legends of a reptilian cavern world called Patalas, etc. – Hitler became obsessed with the novel and was apparently fanatical over the prospect of an imminent underground invasion of the surface world in the future, and wanted to make alliances with these underground races so that once they emerged he could rule the earth in joint capacity.'

Some have offered the theory that these underground beings consist of three main types: humanlike sorcerers, reptilian humanoids who are apparently a branch off from the ancient raptor-type bipedal saurian species who bypassed extinction by escaping into an underground cavern realm, and also short, grayish cybernetic drones.

There are underground bases rumored to exist around the world. For example, there are reports of a Nazi-alien connection/collaboration operating in a massive underground base near or under the Denver International Airport in Colorado. Also, a major control center for Nazi-reptilian collaboration is reported to exist beneath the Gizeh plateau of Egypt, in a strange scenario that seems similar to a cross between the movies 'Stargate' and 'Raiders of the Lost Ark.'

Another rumor about a Nazi underground base claims that the Nazis have infiltrated en masse the cavern systems and ancient tunnel networks left by the Murians and the Atlanteans, which exist below the western United States. The Nazis may also be part of the horror show said to exist underground in Dulce, New Mexico, which is familiar to UFO believers as a joint human-alien operation where genetic experiments are carried out and where attempts to reverse-engineer UFO technology may be taking place, with or without alien help.

'Incidentally,' the posting continues, 'some abductees have been taken to underground bases where they have seen swastikas on the walls, or have seen UFO craft with the same symbol. There are many sources that tend to confirm the Nazi-UFO connection.'

The writer refers to the alien that early abductee Barney Hill encountered along with his wife Betty in 1961. Under regressive hypnosis, Barney is quoted as making the following statement: 'Another figure has an evil face. He looks like a German Nazi. His eyes! His eyes! I've never seen eyes like that before.'

German V2 rocket developer Werner von Braun claimed to believe in extraterrestrials, but could he have been covering for a secret Nazi space program that the U.S. knew all about when they allowed him into the country along with other fellow Nazis under the highly classified Project Paperclip?

WHERE DID THIS KNOWLEDGE COME FROM?

There is of course the question of where this Nazi-inspired UFO technology might have come from. Certainly it's a valid question if one is to entertain the notion that Hitler's rocketry henchmen had a bit more under their V-2 sleeves than we are led to believe.

'Abducted by Aliens' author Chuck Weiss has researched the Nazi occult conspiracy extensively and observes that, as a young man, 'Hitler came under the influence of Germany's darkest occultists, members of the Thule Society and its inner circle of Black Magicians called 'The Luminous Lodge,' although amongst themselves these Magicians referred to their order as the 'Vril Society."

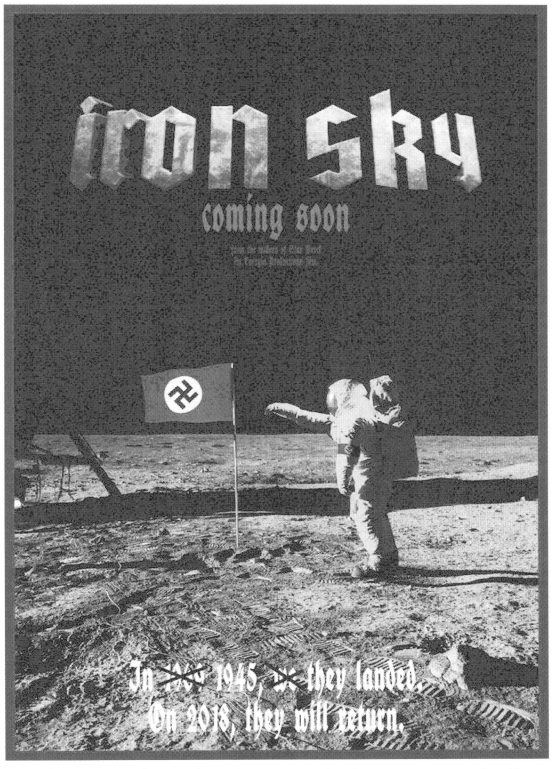

Did the Nazis get to the moon before anyone else?
A conceptual poster from the film "Iron Sky."

This, says Weiss, was the beginning of the twentieth century's 'great struggle between the Light and the Dark, when Adolph Hitler rose to absolute power in Germany and almost succeeded in his attempt to dominate the world. What only a few people understood at the time, and what was never publicly acknowledged, was the fact that the Nazi hierarchy, including Hitler himself, was deeply involved in the practice of Black Magick.' In fact, Hitler himself claimed to have met the 'superman' and stated that he was evil beyond belief!

Did this 'superman' originate on another world or did he pop in from another dimension?

THE BEAUTIFUL MEDIUMS OF THE VRIL

In our earlier published work, ROUND TRIP TO HELL IN A FLYING SAUCER, we approached this subject and put forward a somewhat startling scenario.

They were utterly fetching.

Almost beautiful beyond belief.

A true Aryan's dream.

Even the top-ranking officer of the SS, Rudolf Hess, was smitten, so much so that he listened enraptured as the young mediums formed a séance circle and began to channel communications from an unknown race far removed from the bunkers of Berlin.

Artist and historical architect Jim Nichols of Tucson has examined the role of UFOs and ETs in the formation and development of Nazi Germany, noting: 'The medium Maria Orsic was leader of the Vrilerinnen, the beautiful young ladies of the Vril Gesellschaft. Characteristically they all wore their hair in long horsetails, contrary to the popular short bobbed fashion of their day, claiming their long hair acted as cosmic antennas that helped facilitate their contact with extraterrestrials beings from beyond.'

And furthermore, says Nichols, 'According to the legend of the German Vril Society, a fateful meeting was held in 1919 at an old hunting lodge near Berchtesgaden, where Maria Orsic presented, to a small group assembled from the Thule, Vril and Black Sun

Societies, telepathic messages she claimed to have received from an extraterrestrial civilization existing in the distant Aldebaran solar system, sixty-eight light years away, in the Constellation of Taurus. One set of Maria's channeled transmissions was found to be in a secret German Templar script unknown to her.' When translated, these transmissions held the key to constructing a circular flying craft capable of traveling around the world at great speed as well as exiting the Earth's uppermost atmospheric levels.

The Vril Society was an occult 'Luminous Lodge' that was a sort of inner circle for the Thule society that was in close contact with an English-based group called the Hermetic Order of the Golden Dawn, a magical cabal that had great influence on western occultism throughout the 18th and 19th centuries. The members of the Golden Dawn were Rosicrucians and Masons and it is said they conjured up many an obstinate spirit. The Vril ladies claimed their group was formed as a meditation and mystical society meant to awaken the Vril force or 'prana,' as many would come to call this invisible mystical cosmic force today. Any of the ancillary benefits such as contacting extraterrestrials would come as a bonus . . . a bonus that Hitler and his henchmen became fascinated with as it offered up a potential power comparable – perhaps surpassing – anything being developed by the Allies.

The Vril mediums were perplexed by the content of the messages from off world. One of their order, a psychic known as Sigrun (named after one of the nine daughters of Wotan of Norse mythology), joined the gallery and began to decipher the images being channeled via automatic writing. It is generally thought that the transmissions were strikingly similar to ancient Sumerian.

The Nazi connection to UFOs and alien abduction remains unproven, of course, but we would venture to say that it is a concept that is growing increasingly more popular every day. But it still staggers the mind even to contemplate the evidence of the monstrous Third Reich having such radically advanced science, a technology that continues to lurk in the shadows of the UFO mystery. But if true, some of the signs and symbols of their mastery might already be visible to the naked eye and by looking up at the moon through a telescope. A frightful sight indeed!

THE BEDAZZLING CLAIMS
OF A HACKER

The U.S. government has been trying to have him bought across the pond to the United States to face a serious military tribunal that could put him behind bars for the rest of his life.

Gary McKinnon is a Scottish-born systems administrator and a hacker who has been accused of what one US prosecutor calls the 'biggest military computer hack of all time.' McKinnon has denied the charges, saying he was only looking for evidence of the suppression of free energy and a cover-up of the reality of UFOs as well as for other technologies the public has a right to know about, making him an idealist of sorts in the fight for UFO and secret space program disclosure.

The legal aspects of the case, which as of this writing still have not been resolved, are complicated. McKinnon is accused of hacking into 97 US military and NASA computers over a 13-month period between February 2001 and March 2002, using the name 'Solo.' The US authorities claim he deleted critical files from operating systems, which shut down part of the US military's network of computers for 24 hours. It is also claimed that he deleted files belonging to the US Navy, rendering their computers inoperable after the September 11 terrorist attacks.

McKinnon is also accused of copying data, account files and passwords onto his own computer. According to US authorities, the cost of tracking and correcting the problems he caused was over $700,000.

McKinnon admitted to leaving a threat behind on one computer: 'US foreign policy is akin to government-sponsored terrorism these days. It was not a mistake that there was a huge security stand-down on September 11 last year. I am SOLO. I will continue to disrupt at the highest levels.'

The US, for its part, has declared that it will fight McKinnon's attacks 'as strongly as possible.'

Gary McKinnon and his mother Janis Sharp at the Doughty Street Chambers press conference 15 January 2009.

'We suffered serious damage,' said a senior military officer at the Pentagon. 'This was not some harmless incident. He did very deliberate damage to military and NASA computers and left silly and anti-America messages. All the evidence was that someone was staging a very serious attack on US computer systems.'

McKinnon was arrested in 2002 by the UK National Hi-Tech Crime Unit as well as indicted by a federal grand jury in the Eastern District of Virginia in the US on seven counts of computer-related crime, each of which carried a potential ten-year jail sentence. He could face 70 years in prison in the US, and has been fighting against extradition ever since.

WHAT DID HE ACTUALLY FIND?

With all of that legal drama as a prelude, what did Gary McKinnon actually find when he hacked into the files of the US military and NASA?

According to a 2005 article that appeared in the UK newspaper 'The Guardian,' the following dialogue took place with a reporter.

McKinnon told the reporter that he had done a trial run as a hacker by sneaking into the computer network of Oxford University, which he found, 'incredibly exciting. And then it got more exciting when I started going to places where I really shouldn't be.'

'Like where?' the reporter asked.

'The US space command,' McKinnon replied.

'What was the most exciting thing you saw?'

'I found a list of officers' names,' McKinnon said, 'under the heading 'Non-Terrestrial Officers.' It doesn't mean they're little green men. What I think it means is not Earth-based. I found a list of 'fleet-to-fleet' transfers and a list of ship names. I looked them up. They weren't US Navy ships. What I saw made me believe they have some kind of spaceship, off-planet.'

'The Americans have a secret spaceship?'

'That's what this trickle of evidence has led me to believe.'

IN THE INTEREST OF 'DISCLOSURE'

McKinnon said he was greatly inspired by statements made at a press conference in Washington in May 2001 hosted by 'The Disclosure Project,' which sought evidence of UFOs, antigravity technology and the cover-up of advances in free energy, all of which McKinnon claims to have proven through his actions.

In an interview with the BBC, he also claimed that 'there are some very credible, reliable people all saying that yes, there is UFO technology, there's antigravity, there's free energy, and it is extraterrestrial in origin. They've captured a spacecraft and reverse-engineered it.'

He said he investigated a NASA photographic expert's claim that at the Johnson Space Center's Building Eight, images were regularly cleaned of evidence of UFO craft and confirmed this by comparing the raw originals with the 'processed' images. He also saw a detailed image of 'something not manmade' and 'cigar-shaped' floating above the northern hemisphere. He said he did not think to capture the image for his files because he feared he might be disrupted in his efforts owing to the lateness of the hour and because he was 'bedazzled' by all he was finding. His connection was interrupted at that point anyway, probably because his presence had been sensed by the NASA computer he had hacked into.

In November of 2002, McKinnon was caught, which he says was inevitable because he was 'getting a bit sloppy.' He turned down a plea bargaining deal with US authorities because they refused to put assurances about a reduced sentence in writing.

But if McKinnon's claims about NASA and the US Navy are true, they may serve as concrete proof of some of the mythology that has grown up around the belief in a secret space program. Since McKinnon admits he was usually high on marijuana as he did his hacking work, the Guardian reporter jokes that the US authorities are probably not too worried about McKinnon's claims regarding what he found.

At least for now.

A THERAPIST PROVIDES CONFIRMATION

Dr. Richard Boylan is a behavioral scientist, university instructor, certified clinical hypno-therapist, and researcher into Star Visitor-human encounters. He has maintained a longtime interest in UFOs and associated cosmic phenomena. Because of his affiliations, he has amassed material that would not be easily accessible to others. One of the matters he has found himself confronted with is the possibility of a secret space program. Much of what he has discovered confirms the hacking experiences of Gary McKinnon to the point of revealing the existence of a UFO fleet circling just outside the range of our prying eye but visible to those who know where to look.

'On July 21st of 2011, when Space Shuttle Atlantis landed at NASA's Kennedy Space Center in Florida and headed to a museum, we were told that the U.S. no longer had any space-capable vehicles, and that we would have to rely on Russia and other countries to get into orbit and visit the Space Station.

'That was a lie.

'In actuality, since the late 1980s, the U. S. space fleet has now grown to eight cigar-shaped motherships (each longer than two football fields end-to-end) and 43 small 'scout ships.'

'The US Space Fleet operates under the US Naval Network and Space Operations Command (NNSOC) [formerly Naval Space Command], headquartered in Dahlgren, Virginia. There are approximately 300 personnel at NNSOC's Dahlgren facility. The US Space Fleet's vessels are staffed by Naval Space Cadre officers, whose training has earned them the prestigious 6206-P Space Operations specialty designation, after they have graduated from advanced education at the Naval Postgraduate School in Monterey,

California and earned a Master of Science degree in Space Systems Operations.

'Both the Navy and the Marine Corps furnish men and women officers to this program. Jarheads in space? You betcha!

'Because of its advanced technological position, the U.S. has been designated by Star Nations to provide space security for Earth. This space-security mission is two-fold. One part of the Space Fleet's mission is to prevent rogue countries or terrorist groups from using space from which to conduct warfare against other countries or within-country targets. Star Nations has made it quite clear that space is to be used for peaceful purposes only. The second part of the Space Fleet's mission is to prevent the global-elite control group, the Cabal, from using its orbital weapons systems, including directed-energy beam weapons, to intimidate or attack anyone or any group it wished to bend to its will.

'Because the Space Fleet has the job of being Space Policeman within our solar system, its program has been named Solar Warden. The Space Fleet operates not only with classified U.S. Government authority but also with the secret authority of the United Nations, because the Space Fleet's mission is to protect the entire Earth and all countries. And the Solar Warden program operates under authorization by Star Nations, the organization of advanced intelligent civilizations in space.

'When British civilian Gary McKinnon hacked into U.S. Space Command computers several years ago and learned of the existence of 'non-terrestrial officers' and 'fleet-to-fleet transfers' and a secret program called 'Solar Warden,' he was charged by the Bush Justice Department with having committed 'the biggest military computer hack of all time,' and stood to face prison time of up to 70 years after extradition from the UK.

'But trying earnest McKinnon in open court would involve his testifying to the above classified facts, and his attorney would be able to subpoena government officers to testify under oath about the Navy's Space Fleet. To date the extradition of McKinnon to the U.S. has gone nowhere.

'Lest anyone think that the above is an errant flight of fancy, important corroboration of this information is found in the National Defense Authorization Act for FY 2012, which just passed the Senate December 15 and awaits the President's signature. Section 912 of that Defense Bill refers to the Secretary of Defense purchasing and taking delivery of 'space vehicles."

WEBSITE:
http://www.drboylan.com

"Free Gary" t-shirts and posters are still popular in the UK as friends and supporters try to prevent him from being extradited to the US to stand trial.

NASA'S MAGICKAL MYSTERY TOUR

So you think that NASA is a public servant, whose sole motivation for existing is to serve the American public in matters dealing with outer space and travel between the planets? That they are innocent lambs who have no deceitful interests and are content to aim the Hubbell Telescope and make sure our astronauts are well suited up while in orbit or when on a space walk?

Truth be told, it's an extraordinarily different story.

There is a long list of NASA malcontents who can enlighten you otherwise. We shall, for example, be meeting with the likes of Richard Hoagland, who has been challenging NASA on numerous conspiratorial matters since he left their employ, and the minister Texe Marrs who maintains NASA is fully submerged in the tribulations of Freemasonry and ritualistic occultism and have been since the very inception of the space agency.

Indeed, there are elements of the darker aspects of occultism, ritualistic sex magick and the symbols of Freemasonry throughout the entire workings of NASA, and they don't even try to hide the facts.

JACK PARSONS, AN UNLIKELY SPACE AGE PIONEER

Let's take for example one of NASA's founders and his adherence to the utterly bizarre and downright freaky.

Jack Parsons and the rocket fuel he invented took NASA and the Apollo astronauts to the moon. But his personal life was fraught with strange, even wicked, complications and cast a dark shadow over the entire space program, both public and secret.

According to Reason.com, in a piece called 'The Magical Father of American Rocketry,' Brian Doherty says about Parsons, 'He was an acolyte of Aleister Crowley, an employee of Howard Hughes, and an enthusiastic phone buddy to Werner Von Braun. He became a vital link in two mighty chains in human history: rocketry and ritual magic. His science was built on intuition, and his magic on experiment.'

Parsons was born in 1914, the only child of a broken home, and died in 1952, in an explosion in his backyard lab in Pasadena, California.

BLOWING THINGS UP

Doherty reviews a 2005 biography of Parsons called 'Strange Angel: The Otherworldly Life Of Rocket Scientist John Whiteside Parsons,' which 'tells the bizarre tale of a character whose innovations in rocket fuel design were vital to mankind's leaving the surface of the planet.'

While Parsons had only a high school education, his deep knowledge of explosives, which developed through early issues of 'Amazing Stories' and stints with explosive powder companies, earned him a leading role in a small gang performing rocketry experiments at and around Caltech in the 1930s. At that time, rocketry was for 'twisted dreamers,' not serious scientists. His gang was nicknamed the 'Suicide Squad' because of the frightening explosions they were causing on campus. They were later relocated to the nearby Arroyo Seco canyon to conduct their experiments in discovering stable, usable rocket fuels.

When World War II came along, the US military called upon these oddballs at Caltech, hoping to use their crazy rocket gadgets to propel planes into the air in places without adequate runways.

'Gradually, the little gang of misfits,' Doherty writes, 'evolved into the Jet Propulsion Laboratories. Parsons designed new rocket fuel after new rocket fuel, and eventually they succeeded in inventing jet-assisted takeoff. The military wasn't designed for Parsons' unconventional life- and work-styles. It took staid money boys and military discipline to turn his ideas into an industrial machine.'

John Whiteside Parsons was an unorthodox genius, a poet and rocket scientist who helped give birth to an institution that would become mankind's window on the universe. He was also a devotee of the black arts, a sci-fi junkie and host of backyard orgies on Pasadena's stately Millionaires' Row. ("Life as Satanist Propelled Rocketeer," Los Angeles Times, March 19, 2000)

A LITTLE EVIL ON THE SIDE

While inventing the rocket fuel that would make the space age possible, Parsons also explored the frontiers of inner space, building the other half of his weird reputation.

'He became enraptured with the writings of Aleister Crowley and joined the LA-based Agape Lodge of Crowley's Ordo Templi Orientis. Crowley's American lieutenants seized on the charismatic and successful scientist as a potential savior for their movement; he began donating almost all his salary to the upkeep of his lodge brethren.'

After the war, his occult activism attracted the young L. Ron Hubbard into his life. The pre-'Dianetics' Hubbard took off for Florida with Parsons' girlfriend and most of his money and never came back. The official Scientology version of the story is that Hubbard was sent by Navy intelligence to break up Parsons' evil occult sex ring.

In the late 1940s, Parsons was stripped of his security clearance and almost prosecuted for treason for slipping classified documents from his then-employer, Hughes Aircraft, to the newly established Israeli government, with whom he hoped to work in developing new rocketry.

According to an online posting by Nick Redfern, called 'Final Events: UFOs, Demons and the Government,' the man still so revered and honored by senior figures within the US space program was an admitted occultist who would attempt a ritual to try and invoke the Greek god, Pan, before each rocket test.

When the FBI investigated Parsons following the theft of the classified papers from Hughes Aircraft, they turned up even stranger allegations.

An earlier Air Force report was forwarded to the FBI which related Parsons' experience with Aleister Crowley's followers.

'A religious cult,' the report read, 'believed to advocate sexual perversion, was organized at the subject's home, at 1003 South Orange Grove Avenue, Pasadena, California, which has been reported subversive.'

One of Jack Parson's inspirations was the
"wizard" of the dark arts, Aleister
Crowley, who made contact with
interdimensional beings who very much
resemble the greys of UFO lore.

The Air Force and FBI also had knowledge of the Church of
Thelema, saying 'this cult broadly hinted at free love,' and that there
had been 'several complaints of strange goings on at this home,' and

that an unnamed source had described the church as 'a gathering place of perverts.'

'Women of loose morals were involved,' the report goes on, 'and the story of Parsons' activities had become fairly common knowledge among scientists in the Pasadena area.'

That Parsons had been highly cavalier with confidential files was a serious matter in itself, Redfern goes on. But that Parsons – occultist and perhaps sexual deviant – had been granted a Top Secret clearance was seen as being utterly beyond the pale. His clearance was revoked on the grounds that he might voluntarily or involuntarily pose a danger to US national security.

A LEGACY OF RUMOR AND STRANGENESS

Naturally such a figure as Parsons continues to inspire a lot of rumor and conjecture. Along the way, he has been accused of engaging in sexual bestiality with a dog and ritual incest with his mother. He was also said to have engaged in painstaking rituals designed to create a 'Moon Child,' a magickal being who would usher in a new age of unfettered liberty and signal the end of the Christian era and its 'outmoded' morality. It is an interesting side note that the man who invented the rocket fuel that took us to the moon was also attempting to conjure a supernatural creature named after that same celestial object.

When one factors in the Nazi origins of Werner Von Braun along with Parsons' deep-seated occult connections, it creates a witch's brew of mystery as to the true beginnings of the American space program, secret or public. Was some kind of backdoor deal made with Satan to ensure the US would be first in the race to the moon and beyond? Do we owe it all to a demonic voice whispering in the ears of carefully chosen scientists of dubious moral background?

Naturally, in our eagerness to discover the agents behind the Secret Space Program, if NASA is to be accused of being part of same, we must ask what would be their reason for adapting to and tolerating such weird behavior?

'NASA might have been formed for the specific reason of going to the moon and recovering evidence of whoever lived there a long, long, time ago.' Or so theorizes Mike Bara, who, along with coauthor Richard Hoagland wrote 'Dark Mission – The Secret History of NASA,' a pot boiler on the space agency and its Freemason/Occult connection that landed on the *New York Times* best seller list.

We can't be sure if this is the case, of course, but it does cast an ominous shadow over achievements we are often urged to feel a patriotic sense of pride about, and it certainly gives us food for thought.

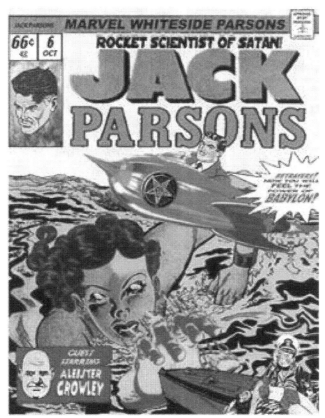

Even Marvel Comics couldn't resist
doing a special issue on the
"madman" who helped found NASA. The
space agency still honors
him every Halloween with an officially
sanctioned occult ritual.

BEDDING DOWN WITH THE MASONS ON THE MOON

Everyone knows someone who is a Freemason. There are millions of members and some no doubt live and work in your neighborhood. They are outstanding members of the community, active in all manner of charity and goodwill. Well, actually, according to some advocates of the Secret Space Program, the Freemasons are a lot more complex an organization than one is led to believe. They are, in fact, a secret, two- layered fraternal order that puts on a positive public face, while at the same time there is an inner tier made up of members that are far from benevolent in their approach to the everyday ways of life. The inner circle of Freemasons is sinister and Satanic and ungodly, or so say some critics, such as Biblical prophecy expert and minister Texe Marrs.

A retired career officer in the U.S. Air Force, Texe has taught American defense policy, international affairs and political science at the University of Texas.

In a feature-length video called **The Eagle Has Landed,** Marrs reveals how NASA and several of the astronauts are actually a front for a group of Freemasons and Occultists who conducted secret rituals on the lunar surface.

The minister Texe Marrs is convinced that there is a dark connection between the brotherhood of Masonry and several of the American astronauts who landed on the moon, bringing a Masonic flag with them.

In the video, Marrs talks about how NASA has embedded numerology, signs of the Zodiac, mythological figures, and the deity of ancient mystery religions in its space program. He points out how the names of NASA's spacecraft and missions demonstrates this – Apollo, Gemini, Atlantis, Columbia – as do the agency's symbols and logos and even the badges and patches on the uniforms of astronauts.. He even professes to have knowledge of the fact that NASA's genetic experiments are responsible for the creation of the monstrous chupacabras seen throughout South America.

MARRS ON THE MASONS

Another Marrs on a mission, bestselling author Jim Marrs, gives us a bit of a historical prospective on this secret order in his book **Ruled By Secrecy.**

'Although the brotherhood of Masonry appears to be relatively new, it is in reality the oldest continuous network on the planet, dating back many thousands of years, beginning when stones were first dressed. Masonry today has a generally sinister reputation, because the people suspect that this powerful brotherhood has been manipulating and exploiting them. However, the average Mason has never been 'in the know' and is, therefore, merely a member of a social club. Nevertheless, the higher-ups have indeed had their hand in creation on this planet on a large scale for a long time ... The Masons are there, perpetually hidden behind the scenes, leaving clues to their existence as a brotherhood, some of which are evident yet still not seen. For example, the biblical Nimrod, the king who built the tower of Babel, is considered the first Mason.'-Acharya S., 'The Christ Conspiracy' (238-9)

Commemorative First Day Letter proves that astronaut Edward Buzz Aldrin was a longtime member of the Freemasons.

Freemasonry is a secret fraternal order that has existed for hundreds, arguably thousands, of years and is now operating in almost every country in the world. Masonry promotes itself as a philanthropic club for men of morals and they perpetuate this image through members of the first three 'Blue Degrees.' Ninety-seven percent of all Masons fall into this category and they are often upstanding citizens, pillars of the community who truly are charitable and benevolent. However, the higher degrees, the inner-circle of World Freemasonry, use the society's global influence to advance their control.

'The ongoing connective tissue between the modern and ancient secret societies has been Freemasonry, which existed as a formidable force long before certain lodges became 'Illuminized.' During the late Middle Ages when any opposition to the Holy Roman Universal (Catholic) church was forced deep underground, among the only organized groups able to move freely throughout Europe were the guilds of stone masons, who maintained meeting halls or 'lodges' in every major city. The masons, who traced their own secret knowledge of architecture and building back to Egypt and beyond, were essential in the construction of Europe's churches and cathedrals. They were the direct descendants of early guilds of masons which existed both in Egypt and Greece and utilized esoteric construction techniques in their craft. These techniques had been passed down through the sects and mystery schools and some continue to confound modern builders.'–Jim Marrs, Rule by Secrecy (242-3)

The highest known formal degree of Masonry is the 33rd degree. This title has been held by many world leaders and important names in modern history. The following US presidents are/were known to be Masons, many of them 33rd degree: Washington, Jefferson, Madison, Monroe, Jackson, Polk, Buchanan, Johnson, Garfield, McKinley, Roosevelt, Taft, Harding, Roosevelt, Truman, Ford, Carter, Reagan, Clinton, both Bush's and Obama.

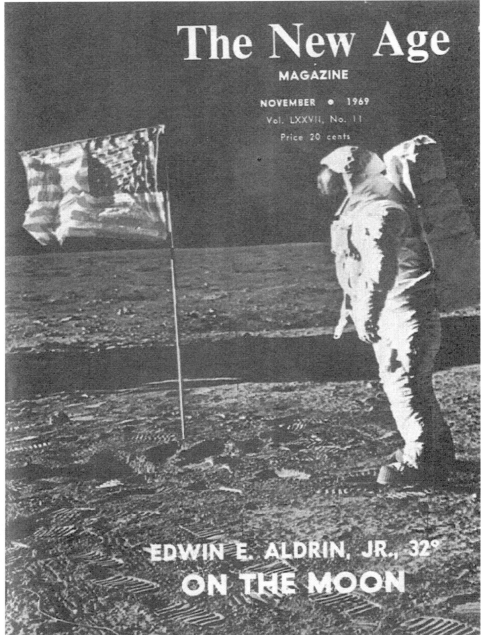

The New Age
MAGAZINE
NOVEMBER ● 1969
Vol. LXXVII, No. 11
Price 20 cents

EDWIN E. ALDRIN, JR., 32°
ON THE MOON

"When man reaches new worlds, Masonry will be there."
The above is a quote from the December 1969 issue of The New
Age Magazine, the official magazine of the Supreme Council 33°
A.&A. Scottish Rite of Freemasonry of the Southern Jurisdiction,
Washington, D.C. Edwin E. Aldrin, Jr., 32°, visited the Scottish Rite
headquarters at the House of the Temple in Washington, September
16, 1969, after the historic moon landing of Apollo 11, and brought
back the Freemasonic flag that he took with him to the moon.

All the following people are/were also Masons, most of them 33rd degree: Buzz Aldrin, John Glenn, Yasser Arafat, Tony Blair, John Wilkes Booth, James Cameron, Winston Churchill, Walt Disney, Bob Dole, Frederick Engel, Newt Gingrich, Mikhail Gorbachev, Al Gore, Billy Graham, Richard Holbrooke, J. Edgar Hoover, Colonel Mandell House, Saddam Hussein, Burl Ives, Jesse James, Jesse Jackson, Henry Kissinger, Vladimir Lenin, Robert McNamara, Karl Marx, Lord Alfred Milner, Benjamin Netanyahu, Albert Pike, Prince Philip, Colin Powell, Cecil Rhodes, James Rothschild, Charles Taze Russell, Joseph Stalin, Strom Thurmond, Leon Trotsky, Paul Warburg, H.G. Wells and thousands more.

'When we examine the historical record of the world's most despicable mass murderers and revolutionaries, we find that almost all of them were members of Freemasonry and other secret societies of the Illuminati: Robespierre was a Freemason; Weishaupt was a Freemason; Napoleon was a Freemason; Lenin was a Freemason; Stalin was a Freemason; Mussolini was a Freemason; Truman and Roosevelt were Freemasons; Ariel Sharon is a Freemason; Bill Clinton is a Freemason; Fidel Castro is a Freemason.'-Texe Marrs, 'Codex Magica' (43-4)

A bit off target, it is still a good idea to set a foundation as to where this is all headed. Apparently, the Secret Space Program is not only secret, but quite evil in intent – otherwise, as Marrs, Marrs and Hoagland say, there would be no reason to keep all of this a secret.

That makes sense – doesn't it?

Hey, somebody has to take responsibility for all the shenanigans that are going on, don't you think? It might as well be a secret society like the Freemasons!

RICHARD HOAGLAND: WHISTLE BLOWER OR MASTER OF DECEPTION?

Richard Hoagland is a proponent of the idea that NASA withholds many secrets regarding a covert space program and that signs of intelligent life on Mars include a very human looking face.

He's about as controversial as a researcher can be.

He's constantly on the backs of NASA officials, accusing them of being behind one hoax or another.

He's a former space agency 'operative' gone rogue. Or maybe a disinformation 'plant' himself working for the 'other side.'

You can hear him on Coast to Coast "... probably more than any other guest.

And he is usually as 'outlandish' as a person can be. But he's calm, cool, well-spoken and knows his subject matter to the point where he is like a steamroller, always pressing his case that there are alien structures on the Moon and a giant face on Mars. He also thinks the astronauts have been subjected to brainwashing to erase what they have seen and might otherwise speak about – that is unless you believe they are members of what Hoagland believes is a super powerful secret society best known as the Freemasons.

He's undeniably a complex individual, in need of close-up examination just as he asks us to do with his cavalcade of evidence in the form of artifacts that he maintains can be seen on the Lunar and Martian surfaces.

Richard Hoagland has for many years been a proponent of the idea that NASA withholds many secrets regarding a covert space program and the presence of aliens in the immediate solar system. While he is frequently sneered at by the mainstream media and scientific community, he is not without credentials establishing his level of expertise.

Hoagland served as a curator of astronomy and space science at the Springfield Science Museum in Springfield, Massachusetts, and was a consultant to CBS News during the Apollo program. He appears regularly as a Science Advisor on 'Coast To Coast "M With George Noory,' and has authored the books 'The Monuments of Mars: A City on the Edge of Forever,' and coauthored the book 'Dark Mission: The Secret History of NASA,' which was ranked 21st on the 'New York Times' Bestseller list for one week in November 2007. His website functioned as 'an independent NASA watchdog and research group attempting to figure out how much of what NASA has found in the solar system over the past 50 years has actually been silently filed out of sight as classified material.'

PHOTOGRAPHIC EVIDENCE

In late 2007, Hoagland released the recording of a National Press Club press conference held on October 30, 2007, in which Hoagland and Ken Johnston, a former NASA employee who worked in the Lunar Receiving Laboratory during the Apollo missions, announced that Johnston was ordered to destroy Apollo lunar images and data forty years previously. Johnston claims that he secretly preserved these Apollo images in a private album, totaling about 1,000 old NASA photos and other pieces of evidence, from his time at the agency. Some of these images as well as Johnston's personal story appear in the 'Dark Mission' book.

The much discussed 'Face On Mars' photograph is part of a city built on the Cydonia Planitia consisting of very large pyramids and mounds arranged in a precise geometric pattern, which Hoagland sees as evidence that an advanced civilization might once have existed on Mars. He believes NASA is covering up the evidence in the belief that publicly acknowledging the artificial construction there would destabilize society.

When the Mars Global Surveyor probe sent back images in 1998 that made it appear that the Face was an irregularly-shaped mountain, Hoagland responded by arguing that the new images were run through multiple filters that degraded the quality of the original image, giving it a cat box appearance which obscures what's really there.

Based on his interpretations of the photographic and other forms of evidence, Hoagland believes that the true color of Mars is salmon red with patches of greenish plant life and a light blue sky; that Mars was once the moon of a larger planet which exploded, leaving Mars isolated; that the advanced civilization on Mars had prior warning of the coming disaster and so escaped in spacecraft to Earth, eventually adapting to the environment and developing into the current human race. He also believes that the numerous unexplained objects photographed around the landing sites of the Mars Rovers are pieces of Martian machinery.

STRUCTURES ON THE MOON

Hoagland openly disagrees with the current scientific body of knowledge regarding the moon and asserts that there are large, semitransparent structures of glass on the lunar surface, which he says are visible in some Apollo photos when the images are digitally manipulated. He further claims that NASA is suppressing knowledge of an ancient civilization that once occupied the moon, and that the civilization left behind some of its technology, still visible on the moon's surface.

He has repeatedly alleged that the twelve astronauts who actually walked on the moon, who would have been well-equipped to verify the existence of lunar artifacts and glass structures, have had their memories of evidence of a lunar civilization selectively deleted with hypnosis. Hoagland also says that one can discern the severed head of a robot in one lunar image that has mistakenly been identified as a just another moon rock.

MORE CONSPIRACY CLAIMS

Hoagland also makes the following conspiracy-related claims:

The United States government has covered up the presence of extraterrestrials.

The space agency murdered the Apollo 1 astronauts.

NASA missions to Mars are a 'well-documented interest of the Bush family.'

There is a clandestine space program which uses antigravity technology reverse-engineered from lunar artifacts and communicated by secret societies.

President John F. Kennedy was assassinated by an agency or agencies opposed to his stated policy of inviting Nikita Khrushchev to create a joint U.S.-Soviet manned lunar effort.

Federal agencies such as the Federal Emergency Management Agency (FEMA) and NASA are linked to Freemasonry.

Certainly anyone interested in a secret space program must examine his

testimonials and analyze his statements. Richard Hoagland remains someone to keep an eye on as the fascinating story of secret cities on the moon and Mars continues to unfold.

Hoagland claims that NASA is suppressing
knowledge of ancient civilizations
that once occupied Mars and left artifacts
behind including what looks like
a piece of machinery in this one photo.

HEIL TO THE MEN FROM MARS! OUTREACH AND DIPLOMATIC RELATIONS

A DIPLOMATIC OUTREACH FROM MARS

Apparently, it isn't just slouches like us who are aware of aliens – or whoever they are, perhaps entities pretending to be aliens – having established bases on the moon and Mars. Talk of such matters has reached up higher than you might suspect, including right up the ladder to the top United Nations authorities – that is, if you believe what our dear friend Steven Omar has to tell us regarding a UN diplomat whose name is unfamiliar to us.

Reports of secret meetings concerning space aliens have been downright hoaxes for the most part -- except for a conference sponsored by the tiny country of Grenada, who invited such luminaries as astronaut Gordon Cooper, astronomer Dr J. Allen Hynek and Mars expert and UFO researcher Dr. Jacques Vallee.

In support of the idea that contact with Mars goes high up in the human hierarchy, Omar provides the story of United Nations diplomat Farida Iskiovet, who in February 1972 investigated UFOs and occupant contacts for the President of the General Assembly. She told Omar and his department agents that she had been contacted by a landed spacecraft from the planet Mars.

'The reported contact took place in the Mojave Desert, in California, in 1971,' Omar writes, 'and made the front page of the major daily Arizona newspaper 'The Arizona Republic."

The Mars contact was also reported in 'The San Clemente Sun-Post' by reporter Fred Swegles, whose beat was President Nixon and his staff at the Western White House.

Farida Iskiovet stated that the alien offered to admit an ambassador to their Interplanetary Confederation in this solar system in exchange for an alien ambassador to the General Assembly of the United Nations. It was an attempt to reestablish diplomatic relations with Earth and other planets that had been suspended in ancient times due to hostility on Earth. However, the terms of this peace arrangement were not acceptable to the Security Council, and the exchange was rejected in a secret meeting.

The president of the UN at the time, Adam Malik, was in favor of the treaty and frustrated by UN attempts to block the exchange, so he and Iskiovet contacted Omar and his people to try to establish a civilian council to mediate between Earth and the Interplanetary Confederacy. The corporate and military-government interests that finance and control the UN did not accept the alien insistence on destroying all weapons, ending all wars and eliminating all polluting fuels, which are all the biggest money interests in the world.

President Ronald Reagan, speaking at the United Nations, conveyed his belief that the next big confrontation would be with extraterrestrials.

SIGNS OF LIFE ON MARS

Omar recounts some of the history of belief in life on Mars. Famous astronomers like Percival Lovell reported huge areas of green vegetation that expanded and contracted with the melting of the ice caps and the four seasons on Mars. In the 1950s, teachers in public schools in America taught students that the temperature at the Martian equator was about 80 degrees. The man some credit with having invented radio, Marconi, published data that he believed he had received intelligent radio signals from Mars.

'For three decades,' Omar continued, 'several astronomers in different parts of the world reported seeing flashing and moving lights on the surface of Mars, some huge explosions and other strange 'unnatural phenomena.' In 1927, the US government carried out a public experiment designed to try to detect intelligent life on Mars by sending radio signals toward that planet and waiting for an answer.'

And what was the apparent Martian response?

'A series of dots and dashes was revealed on a machine capable of receiving Morse Code,' Omar writes, 'reportedly originating from the direction of Mars, and a drawing of a human face on a piece of receiving paper in dots and dashes. This drawing in Morse Code was displayed in the Bureau of Standards in Washington, DC. In 1976, the famous Viking probe was sent to Mars by NASA, and out of over 2000 photos taken of the planet, only a small fraction were shown to the public. Since most of those photos were not released in the news media, were they trying to hide something?

'One photo that was published by the US daily newspapers over a decade later shows what many researchers believe to be pyramids and a huge face carved into the surface of Mars. We have studied other Mars photos showing what appear to be an ancient ruined city, roads, rectangular buildings, and walls. Skeptics say that shadows may make natural objects appear like a manmade structure, yet all the photos were taken at different angles from the sun and the cameras show the exact same objects the same way, ruling out the shadow theory.'

When blown up, many of the photos released by NASA seem to show all sorts of structures on Mars that are unknown to the general public . . . signs of a past or present civilization far away from home.

DID THE MARTIANS COLONIZE EARTH?

Having established that Mars most likely at one time harbored intelligent life, Omar moves on to describe just who that life consisted of.

'The Martians who landed on Earth,' he writes, 'about 11 to 12 thousand years ago, over hundreds of generations, slowly adapted to the lower elevations and Earth's climate as they gradually migrated to lowlands over the centuries to seed the Asian races.'

Omar also believes that Mars was involved in nuclear wars when the Orion Empire invaded our solar system in ancient times, devastating the forests, oceans, rivers and atmosphere on both Mars and Mercury, and causing the destruction of the ancient prehistoric Empire of Atlantis on Earth. The nuclear devastation in Atlantean times was so great that very little trace remains today of that culture. It is also possible that Mars was struck by comets more than once, resulting in yet other cataclysms.

Some Martians chose to move to safety inside their planet, deep underground, rather than to flee to Earth.

'Today, an entire civilization of artificial, dome-shaped, protected underground cities,' Omar writes, 'air-conditioned with controlled climate and connected by tunnels and subways, exist all around Mars. These self-sufficient underground communities grow their own food in artificial food facilities created by their superior technology, mine the interior of the planet, and manufacture spacecraft. Mars is reportedly no longer involved in colonizing Earth or trying to substantially interfere in our affairs like they did in ancient times.'

The underground civilization has no pollution, disease, crime, poverty, political corruption, malnutrition or warfare, and few of the problems associated with Earth civilization. It has been described as a technological, intellectual, scientific, computerized paradise, where emotions such as pleasure, sexual ecstasy, and individuality have been eliminated among the locals. Following leaders called 'Knowers' is the norm, and cloning is the main form of reproduction.

A contrasting estimation of the situation, according to Omar, contends that there are also different races living on Mars. These races originate from other solar systems and are at varying levels of spiritual, technological and intellectual evolution, and regularly disagree on planetary affairs.

The Zeta Reticuli race of small, humanoid gray aliens with large heads, long slender arms and no lungs (they do not need an atmosphere to breathe) have a thick tough skin adaptable to the harsher atmosphere of the surface of Mars. There is also a spiritual civilization on Mars that is so far advanced that the other civilizations cannot interfere with it. The spiritual civilization has very little involvement with Earth and avoids our internal affairs. This civilization vibrates on a higher 4th dimensional frequency than the other 3rd dimensional nations on Mars, and obviously at a higher frequency than we Earthlings, and are thus invisible to our eyes and telescopes and probes.

Does Steve Omar's website contain the truth, or at least some nuggets thereof? That's the sort of possibility we admittedly entertain but of course can offer no proof to support. Perhaps future revelations from a more openly informative NASA will one day offer irrefutable photographic evidence of civilizations on Mars both above and below ground.

Until we get some sort of Disclosure, we will have to somehow inwardly satisfy our personal curiosity about Martians – be they actual aliens, Nazi 'scapegoats' or NASA Freemasons, who we have the opportunity to 'expose' next.

A MARTIAN WANDERER – THE ASTOUNDING CLAIMS OF PRESIDENT EISENHOWER'S GREAT-GRANDDAUGHTER

What proof do we have that she is who she claims to be?

We could be smart asses and say we checked it out on the Internet, but let's be realistic. Just because you've read something in someone's blog or heard them talking on some midnight broadcast doesn't prove very much in this age of cyber fabrication. So this is going to be your judgment call as to the legitimacy of the gal who says she is President Dwight David Eisenhower's great-granddaughter, and if she is really part of some spooky espionage program which allows her to wander about on the Martian surface as part of a shadowy 'Secret Mars Colony Project,' complete with CIA-like handlers.

We first heard of Laura Magdalene Eisenhower when she appeared as a guest on Alfred Lambremont Webre's podcast, aired on ExopoliticsRadio.org. We've always felt you have to take with a grain of salt what these Exo-political folks tend to espouse. Good natured, but not always well informed, they not only believe that aliens are here, but that we should take for granted wholeheartedly that they are our God-fearing equals and should open our homes and hearts to them.

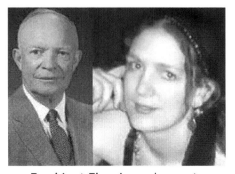

President Eisenhower's great-granddaughter maintains that she has actually traveled to Mars and walked on its surface as part of a CIA-inspired "dark program."

According to what Webre writes on Examiner.Com, "The alleged purpose of the secret Mars colony was to provide a survival civilization for the human race on Earth in the event of a planned (such as HAARP or bio-weapon induced) or natural cataclysm (such as by solar flares) that might depopulate the Earth.'

The Exopolitical chief says that Ms. Eisenhower and a cohort identified as Ki' Lia, a Stanford-educated artist, futurist and fashion designer, have recently found themselves a part of a 'growing cadre of independent whistle blowers disclosing secret technologies and extraterrestrial-related covert operations of U.S. military-intelligence agencies and corporate entities.'

Now this is definitely something ex-governor Jessie Venture should sink his teeth into and expose to the public – one way or another – on his cable conspiracy show. Until then, we can only add to the body of literature, which is ever-expanding, that tells us that the surface of the Moon and Mars may not be as silent as we have come to assume – be they aliens, agents of the New World Order or just a few rogue astronauts thumping around of their own accord.

Three days before leaving office, Ike voiced his concern that that there was a rapidly expanding evil amongst us in the form of the 'military/industrial complex' who endangered our very existence and threatened to actually inject itself into our educational and scientific process so as to push their own corrupt agenda upon an unsuspecting public. Said the former President of the United States, who had led the Allied Forces to victory over Hitler, 'The prospect of domination of the nation's scholars by Federal employment, project allocations, and the power of money is ever present and is gravely to be regarded.'

Laura Magdalene Eisenhower's scenario encompasses so many offbeat aspects, from time travel to the involvement of secret cabals trying to rule our destiny, that it is best in this instance to let the individual tell her story from the outset, in her own astonishing words. We have no other choice, evidently, as it is on occasion a somewhat rambling tale in which one has to read between the lines and connect the dots to fully comprehend . . .

MULTI-DIMENSIONS

Throughout my life I could visualize and feel the larger global energy field, and it was more vast and expansive than I could handle. All global suffering affected me deeply, and I felt an overwhelming responsibility to restore things. The demand was in direct relation to the survival of consciousness on this planet, the survival of my own soul, and the survival of much of humanity in terms of transitioning out of great danger and threats, into our freedom and return to Universal society.

I held a very strong vision of how the world would be if I could retrieve my many aspects that I felt in places other than my body. There was some kind of split that was evident, but it wasn't multiple personalities, it was more an awareness that there was much more to me that I needed to retrieve, in order to feel whole and in order to restore Gaia.

There was so much more needing to be integrated and anchored from the depths of soul and the higher planes of love and light. It was easier for me to journey between the two, rather than be grounded on Earth, because there was a continual attack on my energy field anytime I began to get grounded. I later discovered that it was part of the hidden agendas that I would eventually confront in a very intimate way – one that was trying to force me down a timeline that I wanted nothing to do with.

I knew I was going to be led into that dark realm that is now Hell, but I blocked out the premonitions of how terrorizing and painful it would be. But somehow the Underworld felt like my womb, the region where my creative fires could be awakened to send their transformational love out into the world – to dissolve and destroy evil plots, epidemics and war. That was the part of me that I needed to reach. But it had been taken over and my whole life would be about getting it back.

ENCOUNTERING ATTACKS

My relationship with men began to make more sense in my life, when the Mars recruitment agenda showed up. I had been through a series of events with men throughout this soul-alchemy journey, who seemed to always have some strange relationship with aliens, and if they did not know about it, I could feel a switch go off in some of them at certain times – particularly when I was most vulnerable. I knew this was a lower vibration than our many other allies in the Universe. It seemed clear to me that there were both false abductions (more holographic and communicated to the person through chips), and then there were the real ones – the ones I believe my great-grandfather President Eisenhower confronted, which has been a well-known cover-up.

My life seemed to have taken this legacy on, and although I can't say what exactly happened in the encounter that Ike had, I can say what has been the result of it and the role that I have been given in terms of handling things related to agreements, technologies, battles, and bringing about peace and justice both on and off-planet.

These lower alien entities would lead these men to attack me and be quite out of control. My ex-husband, I came to discover, was giving his sperm to an alien race and had been abducted numerous times. He was very out of control with their frequencies and it was beyond a challenge for me to handle. At night sometimes he would say that he could see them and that they were around us and some nights he refused to even sleep. He had extreme paranoia and shifts in behavior that just happened out of the blue and the erratic nature of his character was very unsafe and at times life-threatening to me. It was sort of by accident that we came together and seemed too random to have been destined, but nevertheless it showed me that something of alien nature was affecting his body, heart, and mind deeply.

Deep down we are all aware of the current global conditions. The limited ways we try to solve these problems never seem to penetrate deeply enough to end the patterns that we are all too familiar with. This felt to me really like the only way – and regardless of that, I didn't have a choice in the matter unless I was going to give myself to those other options that were not in my make-up to even consider.

The only way to grasp what I am sharing is to not only have an open mind, but to look into the roots of how we heal from trauma on a deep level and to view nature as an extension of ourselves as we are an extension of it. Embarking on an archeological dig within could prove useful in creating change, because really the treasures that are lost are in our own being. We can't see this very clearly when our minds are engaged in the dominant powers of control – even if we have grown immune to it and consider our lives content and abundant.

The fact is, the rest of the world is not, and we are all responsible to one another in terms of establishing justice and having the willingness to have compassion and the clarity to see through the false matrix and the devastating effects from it that are taking place. What if we can't do that? Then the outcome is a self-fulfilling prophecy and regardless, all life returns to the great Cosmic womb – and no technology, space-craft, president or scientist can override in words or action – the basic truth of what existed before the big-bang and what is considered the 'Mother of all souls'. The Mother energy is the activator and illuminator of all that has been inherited from her – that resides in our DNA. We are one and we are equals.

I have done incredible work on one level for the organism Gaia, but without humanity joining in with this new paradigm shift – we will continue to live in the symptoms and side-effects of being blind. What is now coming to the surface and all the bliss that is ready to fill the world will only penetrate some, and the gateway that is opening will only be seen by those who have awakened, unless there is a radical approach taken to bring this voice out more.

THE ROOTS OF THE ANCIENT GAME

The Annunaki and all the dynamics related to that race reveal the roots of the Goddess story, and why Inanna (Venus) goes into the realms of Hell to complete this cycle again and again to merge with the dark sister (a part of me) who lay trapped beneath the layers of control. Sacred Union and Hieros-Gamos is also a powerful theme in all of these stories, as well as there being differentiation between the Grail Knights, Shepherd Kings and Christ himself.

At one time the Goddess was in Wholeness, and there was no disease, suffering or war, but the competition between many of the Archetypes and their desire for control splintered the bonds of Sacred Union on Earth, which is the root of all chaos. Different necessities were birthed when the Goddess became split into many aspects, originating with the slaying of Tiamat by Marduk.

Alien energies that showed up in my life seemed to connect to these myths – but I had to understand it as a story in my soul that was helping me to weave myself back together. My work in the world now is to help people understand these concepts so that synergy and a connecting of the dots can be established through all levels of education and awareness, including philosophy, creativity, science, physics, the imagination and the hieroglyphs and archetypes of soul.

In a sense, myth does repeat itself, but like a snowball it grows and grows as we get further away from really giving it the recognition it needs both within and outside of ourselves.

The bond of Divine Union is always intact in the Heavens and creation up to this point has been a long road to weave those polarities back together again in a realm that has severed the bond. This goes from era to era – all holding stories that we have been trying to interpret for thousands of years, like the life of Christ and Eden. Religions are built out of it but there is no direct action in terms of co-creating and getting intimately connected to where Sophia has gone and what she has to say.

NOWHERE TO RUN

After my husband and I began to separate, I somehow accidentally arrived at a psychic institute where more than a dozen readings confirmed my past lives and present energy body. It would truly freak people out if I shared what they told me, so it is better to find some of those things out on my website. I will give some examples though. They said that I was cosmic mind spread throughout the infinite universe. Creation emanated from my senses and emotional body. They saw my root chakra was the planet Earth and they could see the realm above my crown extend to Ain Soph and the unknown God of whom many believe I am the Shakti of.

I had a hard time believing anything that I heard from them so I just listened, but then the emotion would come up and the truth of some of what they said overwhelmed me because I was facing something I could not escape, knowing it was in me. As I was emerging and getting clear validations, books in the mainstream were merging as well, including the Dan Brown novel and movie 'The Da Vinci Code,' which I haven't brought myself to read or see, because I felt something was not accurate.

MEETING AGENT X AND THE MARS MISSION

Timeline

(I will use dates with this since this was the final showdown...)

April, 2006. I decided to go to a festival. I had been such a recluse, dealing with extreme emotions, because I could feel the forces of the archons and negative technologies try to break me on a daily basis. All I could do is cry and scream in absolute refusal of letting any mind control waves into my being. Ki' Lia and I spoke at great length, and I empowered what I saw in her, which was the matrix of Quan Yin and Isis, able to sense the energies in her womb and how it relates to global chaos. After getting to know her more, it was clear that she and I had similar natures as embodiments of Shakti, but with just very different roles.

So at this festival I met a man who we are calling Agent X. We just hit it off and spent the evening together and I was really falling for him big time. I could feel our connection and past lives and just was amazed. I truly felt that I had met my true Sacred Union love. It was miraculous and beautiful and I thought he was so brilliant. He admitted that he was falling fast and it was the sweetest thing ever. We discussed many things relating to Magdalene and Arimathea and how he had heard that our paths would cross, but there was no mention yet of his Mars mission, which would become very intense later.

He seemed to embody Joseph of Arimathea and Osiris in every way and his knowledge of nature, his art work and awareness were deep, intense and quite brilliant. Little did I know he could only maintain his organic nature for brief periods of time, until he was overtaken by something so powerfully corrupt.

June, 2006. We got engaged after some time – after we fully had a heart connection that was undeniable. As I got to know him more he started to reveal things to me about this group he goes to who are quite psychic and deal with alien abduction-related things. He himself had witnessed something truly bizarre with an animal that was skinned and had all the blood sucked out. The radiation or energy around this really affected his health for a long time.

Regarding the group he mentioned, he believed that he had joined a sort of think tank, an investigative group, which was also working on creating a mission to Mars. He kept telling me of the cataclysms that were coming and that this was something we were special to be involved in.

Agent X very much thought that the people he was dealing with were good guys and his physicist adviser was his hero because of the zero point energy and remote viewing stuff he was involved in. He tried to get me excited, saying that we had a chance to escape the disaster. It just did not sit well with me, but he wouldn't talk further, and I just hoped it would all fade away as our love would become much more important. At this time I had no idea the power they had over him, or that they were even using anything on him to keep him as an agent and almost a servant to their mission. I was blinded by love too, and I just wanted to not think about it till it came up again. I later found out that they had sent him to find me.

He knew a lot about me from numerous sources that overlapped with one another – from Freemasons, Knights Templar, to this hidden branch of the government that was behind creating this Mars mission. They understood me based on remote-viewing and time travel devices and they also seemed to recruit people from the Freemasons and Knights Templar who were well aware of the Magdalene path. They seemed to all be connected, but someone was taking advantage of it all and trying to stay one step ahead of how nature may have unfolded as far as us coming together into Union. I did not find out he was an agent until a few months into the relationship, and then I later found out that it was them who sent him to find me.

Agent X revealed to me that they had a list of men who could create that with me and when all of those relationships ended because I broke free and saw through them, they went all the way with Agent X and knew we would somehow meet. They were able to get to him before I was. I picked up on the fact that many have been chipped to destroy me and the energies of the divine feminine, but could never figure out this list and why there would even be one if I was going to eventually meet him. Perhaps as a last resort, as a backup, as a way to reel me in when I had no strength left? There are still many questions that need answering.

I believed I was a person of interest for the agency and was recruited to Mars because of my Eisenhower bloodline. I suppose the reasons were both.

It seemed all these groups were involved with each other without the full awareness of what the agenda was about, except for perhaps one or a few people.

One time he pulled all the equipment in my house apart. Taking cell-phone batteries out, shutting down all electronics – so he could candidly tell me what he knew and revealed much about me and explained why I was even a person of interest. He said that we were being bugged, even with web cams out in the streets, and tried to insist that he was protecting me. What he told me was that this had to do with Sophia-Magdalene and that everything that I knew about myself was indeed true.

If I had it my way we wouldn't be going to Mars, we would stay on Earth and open up a portal (the gateway someone validated that I could open) to a more profound cosmic adventure that promotes freedom for the individual and one's higher abilities as multi-dimensional creators of a divine nature without hierarchy and competition – more love, equality and mutual respect.

August, 2006. The plan was that I would move to Raleigh, NC, and we would live together and figure this entire thing out, as he kept convincing me that my vision and mission would not go unnoticed. So we made the move happen. Upon arrival things drastically shifted. Mars would always come up again, and I was not feeling like it was safe, and I felt that it was a mission being created from a hidden agenda that wished to disrupt our union and have control over it – to be used for their plots in the grander scheme of things, to assist in re-seeding a civilization there. I could just sense it because his behavior often changed and fluctuated greatly from connection with me, to panic and intensity about these missions.

He seemed to have multiple personalities and told me that he did and many had told him that before. He spoke often about alien events that he had experienced and was experiencing. He mentioned that his mother had an obvious chip and I could sense that since he was young, he was being manipulated and his personality was being traumatized by her in order to weaken him to their influence. I began to do research, but then would stop and try to bring him into my world and alert him to what I was beginning to uncover.

REFUSING TO GO TO MARS

Over time, the Mars issue became louder and louder. Ki'-Lia and he were working on plans to make this mission happen, but she realized his plans were dubious based on my observations and could only try to investigate more. She and I would talk more and more, and I would fill her in on my observations. I had dreams and premonitions that something was way off, and in one dream I got taken up by chains into a ship and a voice told me I had to make a choice about being with them or staying on Earth – and that they wouldn't harm me but they would certainly control me.

I chose Earth and fell out of the ship and fell into the ocean and was all alone in darkness. I tried to reconnect with the ship and flew up into the air to just communicate to them and understand things more, but thunder and lightning obscured my ability to see the ship and I fell back into the water. Then some crazy alignment happened and all these planets were surrounding me. This organic light filled my being and I knew I made the choice for Gaia, which connected with my deep awareness of what I am here to create. Plus, I naturally have adverse reactions to being controlled in any way, so I knew it was my only choice.

I told him the dream and he was nervous, but we stayed together and I continued to observe him while feeling a broken heart deep inside. I knew I was losing him to them.

As time went on he would get phone calls and drop everything and do work for some agency. He would say he had to do a mission for them. It started to get more and more intense. All I could think about was this group he had previously mentioned related to Mars. I knew the two were connected but could not understand how something that he thought was so good seemed to involve the ones mind-controlling him and making him do things on their behalf. Something was controlling this venture and it relates to Mars colonies and some sort of off-planet agreement with some of the people I believed he associated with.

I said I did not want to go to Mars even if there were Earth catastrophes, and I felt confident especially after that dream, but he said I had to and if I didn't they would kidnap me. His behavior got worse and worse and he was dealing with all kinds of death threats, and there was no way he was able to pull out of their grips or stay on Earth with me.

January, 2007. I moved down the street and out of the house with him and he would still come and see me. The frequencies coming off him made me physically ill and I realized that they were trying to turn him into some kind of robot. I and a friend of his confronted him, but he got defensive. It was fully clear that he was being heavily mind-controlled. Finally I determined that those he associated with were really up to no good, and I spent a couple of months researching everything associated with Mars and came to discover that a few of them in that group were indeed associated with ELF and HAARP – one even being called the Grandfather of ELF technology. I also discovered a lot about mind control and many other victims and their stories that led to their insanity and sometimes death. I even ordered some rare earth magnets and orgone, to try and de-activate him, but I could never get him to cooperate.

Ki'-Lia and I began to then put the puzzle pieces together more and more, and once she truly got what I was seeing, we began to figure out what the Mars agenda was all about. She agreed with me and began to see the attack that was directly upon my heart. I have had a lot heart troubles in my life and still do.

We discovered that in order for them to have their matrix of control, they wanted the Magdalene-Isis and Osiris seeding of Mars, or the power of the Holy Grail, which means 'royal blood.' After so many readings throughout my life confirmed this as my identity, not just essence, it all started to make sense, but in a way that was hard for me to want to communicate or own up to, except for within. I knew my energy field, heart and intention was strong enough as a personification of the Venus calendar path (which everyone can access) to help regenerate Gaia and Mars and shift us into the positive 2012 Awakening of Consciousness.

I knew this would lead to the liberation from the controls that have kept us imprisoned for so long.

I felt the familiar imprint around me of an ancient Babylonian reptilian entity called Marduk (linked to Mars, Lucifer and other mythological name variations) who is the controller of 3-D Earth and who has been trying to destroy the divine feminine for thousands of years. This is also why the Goddess split into many aspects and had to go into the depths of the underworld to retrieve the dark sister that was being imprisoned beneath – who I in this lifetime would confront as I walk the Venus path like all these other names.

As my own research showed me this and my deep awareness of the dynamic was all too clear, my friend Ki' Lia did research too. But because a book I had written of about 200+ pages disappeared and had been deleted through a rare occurrence that was out of my hands, I will refer to what her research found – since mine is no longer accessible… and this is stated very clearly.

'Marduk is described in cuneiform tablets from ancient Mesopotamia, by the famous esoteric historian Zecharia Sitchin, as the son of Ea/Enki, grandson heir of Anu, and the ruler of the Annunaki or alien astronauts (linked to the Illuminati). He is associated with the hypothesized rogue planet Nibiru (10th Planet or Planet X) or Maldek that was once between Mars and Jupiter. In a mythological battle and astronomical collision with planet Tiamat (or incarnation of Gaia/Sophia), the asteroid belt, the Moon and the Earth were formed.'

Whatever may be going on, chances are when we get to the moon or Mars we will find signs of life -- either past or present -- but will we be told about the discovery, or will the cover-up continue on as it has for decades?

It took all my strength to break free and stand up against this Mars recruitment. They said to him, 'Recruit her and set her up with a handler or leave her,' because his life would be threatened if he left their group and stayed with me. Eventually we split, knowing our connection was a danger, and he knew he was being really messed with too.

After I broke free of Agent X, it was confirmed by a source that Ki' Lia read that the negative timeline had been destroyed, and even renowned researcher/intuitive David Wilcock made that announcement.

WHERE DO WE GO FROM HERE?

We must gather, unite our spirits, dig deeper into our beings to discover the treasures that exist within. WE must empower the fact that we are not separate. We need to open our eyes to the false matrix and the deceits that still linger – and then remove our energy from it and call our power back.

I will be doing events and making myself available, and together we will raise the vibration of the planet through living in the vision and the solution, no longer immersed in the struggles, fears or problems. It is important that we rise as leaders and create action through making changes to lifestyle, self and the way we treat one another.

WE must embrace growth and challenge, and diligently work at creating harmony and equilibrium with all opposing forces. Duality must end, it is time for union. How our roles interact is a dance, not a competition – we must flow and respect diversity and all life forms on planet Earth.

There is still much to uncover and piece together. All I ask is that the secret Mars colony and related issues be further investigated. It is important to educate ourselves on these negative agendas and technologies though because Awareness is Empowerment. There are ways to reduce their effect on our lives, move into nature's will and break free forever from the lies of the false matrix.

I represent a unified field of awareness and my Being affects all. So when I speak, I am speaking on behalf of our divine blueprint and true nature as One . . .

JOURNEY TO MARS
BY
NIKOLA TESLA

TESLA AND THE MARTIAN CONNECTION

Let the truth be known that we have been on top of this discussion for over a decade. It came to our attention early on that there was more activity on the moon and particularly on Mars than could be explained through just abnormal atmospheric activity There seemed to be a "coming and going" which could not be accounted for by simply the NASA-based space program. There appeared to us to be something "weird" and "offbeat" afoot, and we were determined to get to the bottom of the mystery as to who or "what" was responsible for all the reported shenanigans outside our direct planetary influence.

Looking through our files, we can say with certainty that the first massive wave of UFO sightings in modern history was recorded on the West Coast of the United States in and around 1897. Aircraft of unknown origin were beaming down their lights upon cities and landing and speaking with honest Americans.

The aircraft pilots and crewmembers gave a variety of explanations as to their origins. And they seemed to know more about us than we perhaps even knew about ourselves.

Nikola Tesla came to the United Sates in 1884, so there is no doubt that he could have assisted in the design, the liftoff and flight of these great cigar-shaped and blimp-like airborne vessels. Obviously, some sort of technology had to be applied in order for these colossal vehicles to stay afloat and to make it from coast to coast uninterrupted. They did not just "float by" like a balloon. They could freely hover and maneuver of their own devices. They carried occupants that looked like the rest of us. They did not seem to originate from outer space, but they could just as well have gone further than the Mississippi River and traveled on out to nearby planetary bodies.

We don't know for sure that they did, but in this section of our Secret Space Program, which was published previously as **Nikola Tesla Journey To Mars**, we are confronted with a series of puzzles that leave us both pale and with a queasy feeling in the pit of our stomachs.

We agree that in order to fully comprehend the nature of a secret space program – or a breakaway civilization – we must let our thinking wander into the farfetched and the way out.

Truly, there is *something* rotten in the state of Denmark, to utilize an old saying by the Bard. But what that something is we must research further. We are quite convinced that some – if not all – of the answers we seek can be found within the body of these humble pages, though we must search carefully to find them out.

Timothy Green Beckley, Publisher
MRUFO8@HOTMAIL.Com

INTRODUCTION BY COMMANDER X

I Challenge Anyone To Prove
We Haven't Already Been There!

Yes! 'We' have already established colonies on the Moon and on Mars. I can tell you this, because I was once under the thumb of the enemy, having been trained in black operations projects by elements of the New World Order. History tells us that astronauts have walked on the lunar surface, and NASA has sent a probe to the red planet that gave us a 'scientific' bird's eye view of its surface.

This is all part of the 'official' NASA B U.S. government sponsored, and tax payer paid for, space program. But there is another space program that we are told absolutely nothing about. It is a renegade program supported by elements of the secret government working hand-in-hand with New World Order scientists and technicians.

This is why I say 'We,' since the public is not involved and is being kept in ignorance about a potentially important mission that could be of benefit to all of us B but, AS USUAL B is being turned against us by those who would like to keep us in the dark about the actual state of affairs on this planet, as well as in the universe.

As you will see my dear friends, we actually landed on the Moon and Mars a long time ago. Truth is, air travel goes back before the Wright Brothers days, having been rather common among members of certain Secret Societies (various pyramids around the world, for example, contain markings of what are easily identified as flying machines that look remarkably like our modern day aircraft).

This technology – subsequently supported by huge financial contributions from the likes of the international banking fraternal order B has been in place for more than a century and a half, and well surpasses anything that is currently on the drawing boards of the recognized 'establishment.' If we only knew what 'they' have knowledge of, we could toss much of what we have been made to believe right out the window.

Furthermore, you should not be surprised to learn that our old friend Nikola Tesla plays an important role in the development of this unofficial space program...a program that just could lead to further enslavement by our inhumane masters (for more on this topic please read my earlier book *The Controllers*, also published by Global Communications). For it was Tesla who succeeded in the development of anti gravity flight, stolen out from under him by Hitler and other mad power brokers, thus enabling them to 'set up shop' on the Moon and on Mars unbeknown to the rest of the 'free' world.

I guarantee as you turn the pages of this book, you will read about a lot of strange things you may have never known of before. Sean Casteel has done a remarkable job of pulling together the pieces to this puzzle and he should be thanked for doing so. I truly believe it is our given birth right to know the extent of what is going on, in a bid by the New World Order to control the world's population at all cost. For they simply do no wish to share what they know as it would bring peace and stability to the globe; something they cannot tolerate at any cost as it would only go to jeopardize the strong hold they have over us. But, you and I shall fight back as this work testifies we can do.

Commander X

CHAPTER ONE
SECRET SOCIETIES OF THE 1800'S

The modern UFO phenomenon is most often said to have begun with pilot Kenneth Arnold's 1947 sighting over the Cascade Mountains of Washington, from which the term 'flying saucer' was first coined. Arnold's attempt to describe what he had seen, 'They flew like a saucer would if you skipped it across the water,' quickly became a part of the everyday vernacular and set the scene for the thousands of sightings by other observers that were to follow.

What is perhaps less well known is another sightings wave that preceded Arnold and the 20th Century by many years. Beginning in 1896, sightings of mysterious 'airships' were made all across the United States and indeed the world, many of which were written up in the newspapers of the time.

THE STORY BEGINS

According to a book in the **Mysteries of the Unknown** series by Time-Life Books, called **The UFO Phenomenon**, 'Perhaps the most remarkable observations occurred in the United States toward the end of the nineteenth century. Between November 1896 and April 1897, the country reeled under an extraordinary series of sightings that started in the state of California and spread eastward. The wavelike nature of the phenomenon "beginning with a few observations and swelling to a peak, and then eventually subsiding" was to become a regular characteristic of modern UFO sightings.

'It all began on the stormy afternoon of November 17, 1896,' the book continues, 'in Sacramento, the California capital, some fifty miles northeast of San Francisco. A trolleyman named Charles Lusk was standing outside his house and looking up at the roiling sky when to his immense surprise he saw a bright light cruising perhaps 1,000 feet overhead. A faint shape seemed to be moving along right behind it. Others at the nearby capital building glimpsed the 'wandering apparition,' as one newspaper called it, and climbed up to the top of the rotunda for a better view. Another resident claimed to have seen not only the object "which was described as cigar-shaped, with an underslung gondola and pair of side wheels like an old riverboat" but also two men aboard it, peddling furiously on something like a bicycle frame; one of them was overheard saying to the other, 'We will get to San Francisco about half past twelve.' Later that evening, in fact, a similar apparition was seen gliding majestically over San Francisco, flashing a searchlight on the city and sending the local seals scurrying off their rocks into the protective waters of the Golden Gate.'

That report contains so much that is familiar. The commonly reported cigar-shaped craft, the way nearby animals scatter in fear, and even a couple of 'UFO occupants' who seem intent on reaching some kind of destination. And the flap was just beginning.

THE SIGHTINGS CONTINUE

'Over the next two weeks,' according to **The UFO Phenomenon**, 'West Coast newspapers played the story of the mysterious flying machine for all it was worth. Where it might pop up next was anyone's guess. On November 24, witnesses reported it over San Jose as well as 750 miles north at Tacoma, Washington. The next day it was spied over Oakland and Los Angeles, 400 miles to the south. The press was inclined to be skeptical, however. A headline in William Randolph Hearst's **San Francisco Examiner** dismissed the sightings as 'probably due to liquor,' while the rival **Chronicle** suggested caustically that what people were actually seeing was the ghost of Diogenes, the figure from Greek legend who wandered the world with lamp in hand, seeking an honest man.'

Twas ever thus! An unbelieving and 'debunking' media rears its ugly head already.

OF HUMAN ORIGIN?

'Most people, however, seemed to accept the reality of the enigmatic vehicle and believed it to be an airship launched by an anonymous inventor,' the book goes on. 'And considering the temper of the times, this seemed a reasonable enough assumption. The United States was experiencing the first bloom of a great technological era, when anything seemed possible. The electric light, the telephone, phonograph and other recent events were transforming American life. Though it would be another seven years before the Wright brothers' flight at Kitty Hawk, the inevitability of passenger-carrying airships was widely accepted . . . . By the 1890s, Americans and Europeans were conducting well-publicized experiments with manned gliders, and the U.S. Patent Office was flooded with designs for flying machines of both the dirigible and the heavier-than-air types.'

And now the plot begins to thicken a bit as we get a further clue that perhaps there was a human hand behind UFOs, both then and now.

For that, we turn to Jerome Clark's *The UFO Book: Encyclopedia of the Extraterrestrial*. In a section devoted to the airship sightings, Clark writes about a newspaper report that claimed the unidentified flying objects had a human inventor.

According to Clark, '*The San Francisco Chronicle* was headlining the claims of local attorney George D. Collins, who stated that he represented the airship inventor, a wealthy man who had come to California from Maine seven years earlier. Collins was quoted as saying (though he would soon deny it) that he had seen the machine, a 150-foot metal contraption with 'two canvas wings 18 feet wide and a rudder shaped like a bird's tail.' Built in Oroville 60 miles away, it had flown over Sacramento and was now hidden in the San Francisco area while the inventor dealt with some technical problems. But soon he would fly the airship over the city 'a dozen times' and everyone would get a good look at it.'

Unfortunately, Collins was never able to back up his claims satisfactorily and the story began to fade away. However, a short time later, it was reported in **The Oakland Tribune** 'that a prominent citizen, George Carlton, knew the name of the inventor but was pledged to secrecy. He learned it from a fellow Mason 'who talked with the man who saw the machine' as it was tested in the Oroville area,' writes Clark.

While these rumors were never verified, they nevertheless hint at a very human origin for the airships.

HUMAN OCCUPANTS

The UFO Phenomenon has still more relevant information.

'This epidemic of reports,' it says, 'included several cases of reputed face-to-face meetings with a vessel's occupants. A Chattanooga resident told of finding an airship on the spur of a mountain outside the city; a certain Professor Charles Davidson and his crew were making repairs to the craft and told of having sailed east from Sacramento aboard it a month before. A citizen of Harrisburg, Arkansas, also met the crew, which was made up of a woman, two young men, and a patriarchal inventor-captain with piercing black eyes and whiskers down to his belly. The old man, he said, had discovered the secret of antigravity and planned to display the machine in public after flying it to Mars.'

Again you have an inkling to the story this book will attempt to tell: a human source for the mysterious airships that may have already attained the technology necessary to take a manned spacecraft to Mars!

Clark reports still more encounters with human occupants.

In the town of Hawarden, Iowa, on April 11, 1897, 'As a 60-foot-long, cone-shaped airship with four wings passed overhead at low altitude, witnesses heard 'the working of machinery and the sound of human voices, among which was mingled the laughter of women."

Around that same time, in Jacksonville, Illinois, 'Many reliable witnesses assert that they plainly distinguished human voices as a long, narrow, metallic craft with a searchlight flew over town.' Clark writes that human occupants were also seen as well.

Between November 1896 and April 1897, the country reeled under an extraordinary series of airship sightings that started in the state of California and spread eastward.

In Minnetonka, Minnesota, 'Late in the evening a cyclist observed 'a flying machine shaped like an ordinary boat,' with red and green lights on each side and a powerful light in front. Inside the craft were 'living persons, men, women and children. They were moving about as if very busy."

Another sighting of human occupants took place in Danville, Illinois.

'Just after midnight an 'airship' and a smaller 'trailer which followed it very closely' were observed by many residents. 'The ships were of some bright material and the occupants were dressed in western style."

Lyons, Nebraska, was the site of another such observation.

'At 9:30 PM, an airship appeared a mile above the town,' Clark continues. 'It had large fans or propellers that the witnesses could hear. One observer who watched it through opera glasses saw a 'large man muffled in a great coat, apparently presiding over some kind of a steering apparatus."

Finally, there is the story, as related by Clark, of a rabbi's encounter with a human occupant near Beaumont, Texas.

'Hearing that an airship had landed at a farm two miles from town, Rabbi A. Levy went to check out the story. In the darkness, he 'could see very little except the outlines of the ship,' 150 feet long with 100-foot wings. 'I spoke to one of the men when he went into the farmer's house, and shook hands with him. Yes, I did hear him say where it was built, but I can't remember the name of the place or the name of the inventor. He said that they had been traveling a great deal and were testing the machine. I was so dumbfounded that I could not frame an intelligent question to ask."

So there we have eyewitnesses to human occupants, and those occupants further testify to a human inventor!

'Sightings petered out toward the end of April,' the Time-Life book says. 'As one of the oddest episodes in American history came to an end, people were just as mystified about its true nature as they had been at the beginning.'

The preceding has been an account of the UFO/airship flap of 1896-97 based on witness and newspaper accounts of the time. Next, we will move on to discuss what may have been a secret hidden deep beneath the surface of the story as perceived by the public and the media.

MYSTERIOUS SCRAPBOOK

According to the recently revealed private notes of Emmy Award-winning television journalist, paranormal researcher and author Tim Swartz, whose book *The Lost Journals of Nikola Tesla* has become a pop culture bestseller, the entire episode may be only the visible tip of an iceberg that involves not only a secret society, but the legendary inventor Nikola Tesla as well. Swartz is a major player on the conspiracy scene today and goes to great lengths to fill in the gaps, and so we will be hearing from him throughout this book.

'During the 1850s,' Swartz writes, 'mysterious 'airships' regularly crossed the skies of Germany. And just before that, in the year 1848, a young German named C.A.A. Dellschau (1830-1923) immigrated to the United States. Dellschau's own testimony places him in Sonora, a California mining town, in the 1850s. Where he might have been in the decades after that is unknown. We do know, however, that at about the turn of the century, he married a widow and took up residence in Houston, Texas, where he lived in isolation. He had no friends; by all accounts his quarrelsome disposition kept everyone at a distance.

'Dismissed as an eccentric by the few who knew him,' Swartz's notes continue, 'Dellschau devoted hours to the compilation of a series of scrapbooks filled with clippings, drawings and cryptic notations. He died at the age of 92. Were it not for a chance discovery many years later, Dellschau's life would have gone unnoticed.

Eleven of these scrapbooks were discovered in a local dump by Fred Washington, who described himself as a scrounger. The scrapbooks sat in Washington's furniture and antique shop gathering dust until some University of St. Thomas students happened on them. Two books were selected to be part of their display, 'The Sky is the Limit.'

One day in May 1969, a Ufologist named P.G. Navarro happened to stroll past the exhibit at the University located in Houston. Dellschau's two large scrapbooks caught his eye and he stopped to take a closer look.

'Navarro found that the scrapbooks contained old news stories and articles about the attempts of various inventors to construct heavier-than-air flying machines. But these were not nearly so interesting as Dellschau's drawings and notes of strange-looking, cumbersome vessels that he claimed actually had been flown at one time. Navarro eventually talked with Dellschau's stepdaughter, then an old woman. Finally he set out to make sense of Dellschau's notes, which had been penned in English, German, and code. When he had finished, he had reconstructed an incredible story.'

Swartz went on to fill in more details.

'One thing was obvious,' he says. 'Dellschau was of two minds about what he was doing. On one hand, he wanted his 'secrets' known; on the other, he seemed afraid to speak directly. So he compromised and wrote in a fashion aimed to discourage all but the most determined investigator --and even so his writings in the main only add to the mystery. He was writing for an audience-- if not one in his own day, one in some future period.'

Swartz quotes an obscure, almost Nostradamus-like, bit of poetry left behind by Dellschau that went like this: 'You will . . . Wonder Weaver . . . you will unriddle these writings. They are my stock of open knowledge. They . . . will end like all the others . . . with good intentions, but too weak-willed to assign and put to work.'

A SECRET SOCIETY'S AIRSHIPS?

Swartz goes on to reveal that, 'From the notes, Navarro learned that in the 1850s, Dellschau and a group of associates, about sixty in all, gathered in Sonora, California, where they formed an 'Aero Club' and constructed and flew heavier-than-air vehicles. They worked in an open field near Columbia, a small town near Sonora. (Today an airstrip covers the field, the only area in the predominately hilly region where planes can take off and land safely.)   The club worked in secrecy and its members were not permitted to talk about their activities or to use the aircraft for their own purposes. One member who threatened to take his machine to the public in the hope of making a fortune died in an aerial explosion-- the victim, Dellschau hints, of murder.'

There were other instances of members being disciplined for breaking the group's rules.

'Another, a 'highly educated mechanic' identified as Gustav Freyer, was called to account by the club for withholding new information. Apparently this was no ordinary social group. The 'Aero Club' was a branch of a larger secret society whose initials Dellschau gives as 'NYMZA.' He says little about the society except to observe that in 1858 it was headed by George Newell in Sonora. Otherwise, he alludes to orders from unnamed superiors who were overseeing the club's activities. These were not governmental authorities, for Dellschau writes that an official who somehow learned of their work once approached club members and tried to persuade them to sell their inventions for use as weapons of war. The unnamed superiors instructed the club to refuse the offer.

'The club had a number of aircraft at its disposal. However, from Dellschau's drawings, it is hard to believe that anything resembling these machines ever could have flown. Navarro remarks, 'The heavy body of the machines seems to be radically out of proportion to the gasbag or balloon which is supposed to lift the contraption. Considering the large amount of gas that is required to lift one of today's dirigibles or even a small blimp, it is inconceivable that the small quantity of gas used in Dellschau's airship would be sufficient to lift it."

NEGATE WEIGHT OR ANTIGRAVITY FLIGHT

But Swartz adds a wrinkle here that keeps the story afloat.

'This wasn't ordinary gas, however. According to Dellschau, it was a substance called 'NB' which had the capacity to 'negate weight.' Incredible as it may seem, he is talking about antigravity. Still, Dellschau's notes have a curiously pessimistic tone. One strange paragraph reads, 'We are all together in our graves. We get together in my house. We eat and drink and are joyful. We do mental work, but everybody is forlorn, as they feel they are fighting a losing battle. But little likelihood is there that fate will bring forth the right man."

From ***Thy Kingdom Come*** March/April 1959-
Amalgamated Flying Saucers Clubs Of America.

DID SPACESHIPS VISIT EARTH IN 1896?

The following story is reprinted from the Fall 1958 issue of "The Feather River Territorial", P.O. Box 768, Oroville, Calif., James Wm. Lenhoff, Editor, 35¢ per copy, and is herein reprinted through their permission and courtesy.

by James Lenhoff

1896 WAS AN EXCEPTIONAL YEAR FOR WORLD CHANGES AND SCIENTIFIC ADVANCES. BUT THE MOST SPECTACULAR STORY BY FAR WAS THAT OF

The INCREDIBLE AIRSHIP From TABLE MOUNTAIN

The Airship made newspaper headlines for weeks then vanished as suddenly as it had appeared.

Thanksgiving week of 1896 was almost totally overshadowed in California as newspapers from one end of the state to the other carried headline stories about a strange airship which had been observed transcending the evening skies like a prehistoric bird. If these reports were true it was the first time in history that an aircraft heavier than air had flown successfully under its own power.

Through an alert reporter, the *San Francisco Call* managed to scoop its rival newspapers with a full front page account on Thursday morning, November 19th, titled "Strange Craft of the Sky." Both the *Chronicle* and the *Examiner*, jealous of the *Call's* fabulous story, lambasted the veracity of the report and said it was a pure hoax. However, when their offices were flooded with irate citizens who claimed they saw the airship with their own eyes, the publishers calmed down quickly and determined to take the story seriously.

However, even the *Call* was unable to gather anything tangible as to who was really behind the incredible phenomenon. As more and more reports poured in from reputable citizens, including Mayor Davies of Oakland and Mayor Sutro of San Francisco, a solution was in even more demand. Because of the rising political squabbles between Spain and the United States, the federal government assigned its top investigators to determine whether or not the "flying object" was an enemy craft. And, when writers put forth the idea that airships could easily fly over the Sierra Nevadas in a matter of hours, carrying passengers and cargo galore, the monopoly magnates of the Southern Pacific Railroad suddenly turned pale and assigned their best detectives to find out who built the ship and buy him out at any price.

Contemplation of the mystery airship caused many editors to visualize a glowing future which actually was not far from correct. For example, Mr. John Apperson, editor of the little *Willows Review* wrote, "If all is certain that has been claimed, California will bear the proud distinction of having a genius within her borders who has made the first successful flying machine, for it goes against the wind with greater ease than a bird, and is fashioned after the shape of a condor of the Andes.

"With the advent of this flying machine comes the solution to the mystery of a visit to the north pole; air navigators can make a tour of the world - not in 80 days, but in a week. It will meet with no impediments, like unto the vessels that plow the deep, or the railroad train that crosses the raging stream, but will glide along rapidly through every atmosphere congenial to the flight of a bird. It will be useful in battle to observe the enemy's camp or drop dynamite bombs into a hostile camp. To take it all in all, the flying machines and airships are necessary appliances among the rapid inventions of the nineteenth century. Man has chained the lightning and brought it as a captive into our homes, and now, he poses as a competitor and rival to the flight of the largest and swiftest birds."

The strange interlude got started on the evening of Nov. 18th, a Wednesday, when hundreds of citizens of Sacramento saw a dark object in the sky with a huge and powerful searchlight which cast a bright ray upon the ground. The time was between 6:30 and 7:30 p.m., and several persons said they heard voices singing and observed the vessel moved slowly and with a rocking motion. Apparently the ship was cigar-shape with four large wings that were "worked by compressed air." The body of the ship was supposedly made of aluminum and a powerful searchlight on front and bottom was produced from electricity. No one really got a good look at the ship, however, since the great light obscured their view.

A score of citizens watched with incredulity as the ship hovered over the golden dome of the State Capitol, then rose swiftly and headed south toward San Francisco.

The following Monday evening downtown Oakland was tossed into a complete traffic jam when buggies, street cars and pedestrians came to an abrupt standstill as the "monster of the air" swooped over the city, casting its bright electric light upon the buildings, then departed toward the bay. People sat on roof-tops that whole night,

The Airship That Passed Over Sacramento Tuesday Evening, as Described by Scores of Eye-Witnesses.

This cut appeared on the front page of the "San Francisco Call" on Thursday morning, November 19, 1896.
It heralded the beginning of one of the most amazing and still unsolved news stories in the history of
western journalism.

weathering rain and cold winds hoping to get just a small glimpse of the wonderful invention if it should return.

On that same evening the citizens of San Francisco scrambled to the windows and roof-tops as the phenomenon drifted over their city. Mayor Sutro confirmed the story himself by stating that the object was observed by his entire household moving in from the ocean toward his manor which was on Sutro Heights. When it got over Seal Rock it played the searchlight on the seals and they dove into the surf, making all sorts of frantic noises. It flew over the Heights and a few moments later was seen near Twin Peaks, where cable cars slammed on their brakes as passengers piled onto the streets to better view the "glowing giant." At 9:15 p.m. several citizens reported that the airship hovered over Van Ness Avenue about 400 feet off the ground, then rose high above the city and headed over the Ferry Building toward Oakland. A special meeting of the Board of Supervisors was called the next morning as riotous citizens clamored for an explanation.

Finally the *Call* tracked down a lead which at least partially explained who was behind the mysterious happenings. Mr. George A. Collins, a prominent San Francisco attorney, stated that he had been engaged by a San Francisco man to secure the patents on a flying machine which he had built in the rugged seclusion of Table Mountain above Oroville. Collins said he could not divulge the name of his client. The whole thing was to remain a secret until the patents had been secured, but the *Call's* premature story had spoiled the full impact the inventor had hoped for. The man on Collin's list of clients who most logically fitted the description was Dr. E. H. Benjamin, a handsome bachelor, thirty-four years of age who was practicing dentistry in San Francisco. He was an inventor of sorts and admitted that he had a wealthy uncle in Oroville to whom he had been paying frequent visits recently .

When confronted by reporters late at night he denied having anything to do with the invention. However, in a subsequent interview he indicated that he had been "casually" working on an idea for an airship, but that even if he was the inventor, he would be a fool to admit it publicly.

Overnight Oroville had become the celebrated focal point of a national investigation, and the citizens glowed with town pride. Living up to the rivalry which existed between the two towns, the *Marysville Daily Appeal* noted with sarcasm, "Oroville has been credited in times past with giving to the world strange and novel ideas, but no one ever supposed that the "immortal fame" which the denizens of that town have always claimed would one day come to them, would arise in the form of an airship. The story that has now probably been telegraphed broadcast over two continents is to the effect that one of the many Oroville millionaires has at last perfected a machine that will fly through the air. One never can tell what a day may bring forth. Yesterday, Oroville was a struggling hamlet; today it is the home of millionaires and airships."

Exploring parties composed of detectives, reporters, and government agents set out daily from the streets of Oroville to comb the rugged canyons of Table Mountain in an effort to locate the building site, but they returned tired and shabby at the end of the day. It was hard to find anyone in Oroville who would not testify to having seen the airship ascend from over the great gold infested mountain and fly over their town at least once during the past few weeks. However, even R. S. Boynton, editor of the *Oroville Register* said he had no clues except one which might solve the riddle. The only thing he could figure out was that the phenomenon was possibly the work of Portuguese in the mining town of Cherokee which was located on top of the Table. In the early 1880's he remembered that a large Portuguese population had worked the hydraulic bluffs in the vicinity and celebrated special occasions with the ascension of large baloons with huge torches blazing from long ropes which dangled beneath. These would drift down off the mountain and float over the valley floor, usually burning out before they reached Marysville. However, a check on the town revealed there were no more Portuguese left, and the citizens said there was no evidence to support the claim that someone else might be doing the same thing. Besides, the light was of such intensity that no torch could duplicate it.

THE INCREDIBLE AIRSHIP FROM TABLE MOUNTAIN

On Monday morning, November 23, 1896, a slightly different conception of the airship appeared on the front page of the Call. The caption read, "The Great Airship That Is Startling the People of Many Cities. . . .Drawn from description of the inventor's attorney, George D. Collins."

William Bull Meek, popular pioneer at Camptonville, further confused the issue when he wired the *San Francisco Examiner* that an airship landed near his town and five young men went to investigate. They reported talking with a man who answered their questions with alphabetical letters, since he could not hear or talk. He said the ship had come from the Montezuma mountains. By now even Sherlock Holmes would be running around in circles and mumbling to himself.

George Collins almost didn't get any sleep nights, trying to avoid reporters and detectives, and one government agent threatened to arrest him for treason unless he divulged the full story. "I don't know anymore about it than you do," he would constantly reply. "All I know is that a client says he has flown the machine over the state, that it was built above Oroville for secrecy, financed by his wealthy uncle, and I will apply for a patent as soon as a few minor adjustments are made to make it more steady in flight."

And so went the merry-go-round day after day. And with each day the stories circulated over bar and dinner table became more alarming and fantastic.

On December 5, 1896, a front page headline in the *Marysville Daily Democrat* started the furor up with new intensity. The headline read, "It Is Coming!" A letter followed which announced simply, "Weather permitting, we expect to leave Oroville Sunday at 7:o'clock p.m. and should fly over Marysville at 7:30 p.m." It was signed by the Northern California Air Ship Co.

Excitement was in the air, and on Sunday evening the citizens of Marysville were joined on their roof tops by a slew of reporters and interested agents. However, the ship failed to appear, and the following day the *Democrat* ran another front page article titled, "Pirates of the Air - - Airship Scheduled for Marysville was Waylaid in Heavens above Honcut. - - a letter from the Captain."

There followed a lengthy explanation of such imaginative proportion that there was little doubt that the notice had been a prank. It stated that a hot air balloon was sighted by the crew of the airship near Honcut and

as they got closer they saw three men in a basket. They flashed on their super search light and recognized them as antagonistic reporters from San Francisco's *Examiner* and *Chronicle*. With their X-ray machine they saw salt bags on the floor of the basket. As the airship maneuvered underneath the balloon the men dropped the salt on their tail mechanism and rendered the steering gears useless. Then they heaved over two huge grindstones which smashed on the prow of the ship but did little damage. However, when they threw copies of the Thanksgiving edition of the *Marysville Appeal* overboard, they struck in the rotary wings and the plane was grounded. The letter was signed by "Sea Sick Boynton", captain pro-tem of Airship "Register." He added a postscript that Major Frank McLaughlin, mastermind gold promoter of the Feather River, was the permanent captain but that he had left Oroville that morning in his private ship for Canton to aid President elect McKinley in his California appointments. Obviously Boynton was having a little fun with his satire, but a good many persons who sat up all night on Marysville's roof tops did not quite see the humor involved, least of all the angry reporters from San Francisco.

Because no one could seem to track down a lead which got anywhere, and because Collins and Benjamin continued to remain adamant on the subject, interest in the airship was gradually relegated to the inside pages of the newspapers. As the Spanish-American War loomed more acutely as a reality in national affairs, the story was soon completely forgotten.

Was there really an airship, or were the citizens of California having wild hallucinations? Was the whole thing an incredible prank of international scope, or did someone actually produce the greatest invention of the nineteenth century? To this very day, the biggest news sensation since Fulton's steamboat has never been solved.

The Mysterious Flying Light That Hovered Over St. Mary's College, Oakland, and Then Started for San Francisco. It Is Exactly Like That Described by Sacramentans, and Similar to the Cut Published a Few Days Ago in "The Call" From a Description Furnished by One Who Saw It.

CHAPTER TWO
ENTER THE NAZIS

To further lay the groundwork for the revelations to be made in this book, it is now necessary to provide some information about the involvement of Nazis and their wartime technology, much of which was revealed only after the war had been won and the German enemy vanquished.

Did Nazi scientists develop flying saucers of their own? Did the technology that drove the airship flap discussed in the last chapter progress to the point where heavier-than-air 'UFOs' took to the skies with all too human inventors as their original source? These kinds of questions still elude any kind of definitive proof, but we can at least examine some of the more educated speculation now available.

UFOs BEHIND ENEMY LINES

For instance, the legendary Commander X, who has given his support to this volume by contributing material from his personal files, is a former military intelligence operative and the author of many books on conspiracy theory and UFOs. Commander X wrote an article that appeared in a Special Edition of **UFO Universe Magazine: Conspiracies and Cover-Ups** in which he grappled with those very questions and provided at least partial answers to the mysteries they imply.

According to Commander X, 'Nazi Germany's Advanced Secret Weapon and Space Program began in the early 1940s and involved the development of the 'Flugelrad' or 'Wingwheel.' The Flugelrad was a saucer-helicopter, the first vertical takeoff flying vehicles developed by the Nazis. The wings (blades), which issued from the center of the craft like spokes toward the outer rim, were tillable. This was allegedly the 'Model T' of a series of German 'disc' or 'saucer' designs that followed. Much of this program, of course, was top secret even to the German public. According to 'Samisdat

Publications,' an ultra rightwing organization based in Toronto, Canada, the Nazis did indeed develop such a flying device.

'Why then,' Commander X asks, 'did the world not learn of such a thing when Nazi Germany fell? Well, says Samisdat and others, as the war was ending several colonies of German scientists were transported to secret bases in Antarctica and elsewhere (a possibility that, when considered, seems to be plausible) where the secret 'disc' technology was

perfected. Due to the lack of verifiable proof of such an operation taking place, we cannot fully confirm this, but perhaps other documentation will come forth in the future and time will tell whether these claims are legitimate or not.'

NAZIS AND THE OCCULT

Commander X also addresses the Nazis devotion to the occult, and quotes a researcher whose pseudonym is Jason Bishop.

'All of the Nazi-occult groups were more or less closely associated with the powerful and well organized 'Theosophical Society,'' Bishop explains, 'which added to neo-pagan magic an oriental setting and a Hindu terminology. Or, rather, it provided a link between a certain oriental Satanism and the West. Nazi occultism was a mixture of influences and host of interrelated secret societies, including the Bavarian Illuminati, the Knights Templar, the Teutonic Knights, the 'holy' Vehm, the Golden Dawn, the Rosey-Cross, the Vril Society, the German Order and it's offshoot The Thule Society. That last was founded in 1918.

'This was a neo-Gnostic racist group,' Bishop continues, 'which became a rallying front for the secret society roots of Nazism. The chief architect was Baron Rudolph von Sebottendorff (Rudolph Glauer) who had direct contact with the Dervish Orders and knew a great deal about Islamic mysticism, particularly Sufism in all its aspects. He also had contact with Herman Pohl, leader of the German Order Walvater of the Holy Grail.'

Bishop reports that Sebottendorff wrote a book called **Before Hitler Came** that listed the occult affiliations of the Nazi leadership.

However, the Nazis suppressed and destroyed the book, having determined that the information should be kept from the German public.

There were also others whose occult involvements could be nailed down as fact. For instance, according to Bishop, 'The Thulist, Dietrich Eckart, is believed to have initiated Hitler into various occult mysteries with the aid of psychedelic drugs. The most prominent member of the Vril Society was Karl Haushofer, a close confident of Hitler, Hess and Rosenburg. Alfred Rosenberg and Adolph Hitler himself belonged to the Thule Gesellschaft. So did Rudolph Hess.'

From this diverse group of politicians and occultists came the driving force behind the alleged UFO technology of the Nazis.

NAZIS ACHIEVE RESULTS

Commander X then picks up the story again.

'One of the scientists involved with the early Nazi 'saucer' projects,' he writes, 'was of course Victor Schauberger, who was brought to America after the war where he was

rumored to be working on a top-secret 'flying disc' project in Texas for the U.S. Government until his death in 1958. It is said that some of the prototypes, which the government is now developing, are as advanced (wherein propulsion, etc., is concerned) over the Schauberger models as the Space Shuttle is over the biplane. 'Samisdat' relates some information on Schauberger, who might have been considered the aeronautical 'Einstein' of his time, although not nearly as well-known as the famous white-haired Jewish scientist.'

The following is a step-by-step progression of the Nazis attempts, perhaps successful, to develop a disc-shaped aerial craft.

> 'Model I—The most conventional design, by today's concepts. It used a standard German Walther Rocket Engine and was steered by a conventional rudder.

> 'Model II—An improvement over Model I, with a radical departure: A specially designed §rotary wing' stabilized

and steered the craft. This model was more maneuverable and faster.

'Model III—Extremely fast, using a jet-vacuum propulsion system. Capable of attaining speeds of over 6,000 kilometers per hour. The fuel mixture produced vapor trails, an acrid smell, and sometimes flames and sparks. The saucer's propulsion system produced high-pitched whining sounds. The craft was capable of terrific acceleration or steady hover. It could climb and bank steeply and often startled the observer with loud sonic booms as it accelerated through the sound barrier.

'Successors of Model III, still in the planning stage during the mid-1940s, utilized the Earth's magnetic field in their propulsion systems.

'The Schauberger Models—Using the original implosion-powered propulsion system, these Nazi saucers made no sound. They were flameless and smokeless, but the outer skin of the hull, composed of a secret alloy called 'impervium,' pulsated with various colors as the craft sped through the sky at velocities in excess of 10,000 kilometers per hour. Extremely maneuverable, these saucers, dubbed §Foo-Fighters' by Allied bomber crews, could change altitude and course with surprising suddenness.'

THE FOO-FIGHTERS

Later in that same article, Commander X provides even more information about the Nazis and their wartime experiments with flying saucers. This time, Commander X quotes a British writer named Peter Brookesmith, author of *UFOs, Where Do They Come From?* (published by MacDonald & Co, London, England). Brookesmith, says Commander X, 'elaborates on the history of one of the German scientists involved in the top secret Nazi saucer projects. In reference to this scientist, Rudolph Schriever, Brookesmith reveals: 'His 'flying disc' had been ready for testing in early 1945, but with the advance of the allies into Germany, the test had to be canceled, the machine destroyed, and his complete papers mislaid or stolen in the chaos of the Nazi retreat, so the official story goes.

By the end of the war the Nazi's had developed a number of controversial aircraft, including the Andromeda B a large mothership-type craft capable of escorting a large number of personnel to other worlds.

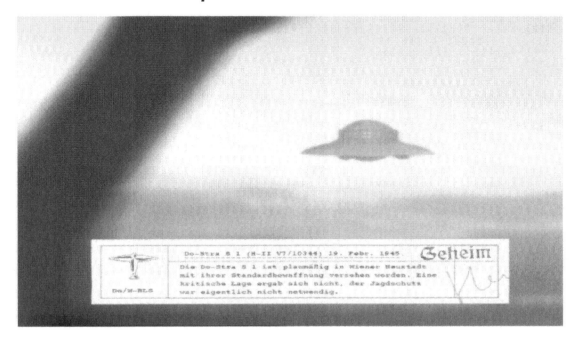

'Schriever died not long after these revelations,' Brookesmith continues, 'convinced that the UFO sightings since the end of the war were proof that his original ideas had been taken further with successful results. But what were the Foo-Fighters? An identification was proposed by an Italian author, Renato Vesco, in a book first published in 1968.

'According to him, the Foo-Fighter was actually the German FEUERBALL (Fireball), first constructed at an aeronautical establishment at Wiener Neustadt. The craft was a flat, circular flying machine powered by a turbojet. It was used during the closing stages of the war both as an antiradar device and as a psychological weapon. Vesco says, 'The fiery halo around its perimeter-- caused by a very rich fuel mixture-- and the chemical additives that interrupted the flow of electricity by over-ionizing the atmosphere in the vicinity of the place, generally around the wing tips or tail surfaces, subjected the H2S radar on the plane to the action of powerful electrostatic fields and electromagnetic impulses.'

'When World War II ended,' Brookesmith went on, 'the Germans had several radical types of aircraft and guided missiles under development. The majority of these were in the preliminary stages, but they were the only KNOWN craft that could ever approach the performance of the objects reported by UFO observers.'

Could it be that the Nazis really had created flying saucer type craft capable of the mind-bending aerial maneuvers that witnesses have sworn to over the many years since? It is generally assumed that the sudden changes in speed and direction UFOs often display would kill a human pilot. But did the German scientists somehow find a way around those technical complications?

BRINGING IT ALL BACK HOME

The previous material by Commander X offers a fascinating glimpse into possible German wartime 'flying saucer' technological advances, but there is another facet to the story that must be examined as well: the postwar efforts of the U.S. government to import Nazi scientists and thus glean vital new defense secrets kept hidden during the war years.

For this we turn again to the venerable Tim Swartz, a journalist and author with many books on conspiracy and secret science research to his credit. In an article, '***The Fourth Reich and Operation Paperclip,***' Swartz lays the whole dirty secret bare and explains how the business of defense research often makes for strange bedfellows.

'At the end of World War II,' Swartz begins, 'Europe lay in ruins. The Axis Powers had been defeated and the United States and Soviet Union emerged victorious as the world's new superpowers. Despite their unified and successful goal of defeating Hitler's Germany and the evil Nazi empire, America and Russia still carried a deep-seated mistrust for each other that soon rekindled and nearly ignited several times over how to deal with a postwar Europe.'

America and Russia's response, as reported by Swartz, went like this:

'In 1945, intelligence teams from the superpowers began a hunt throughout occupied Germany for military and scientific riches. They were searching for scientific achievements like new rocket and aircraft designs, medicines, and electronics. However, they were also hunting down the most precious item of all, the scientists, engineers and intelligence officers of the Third Reich whose work had nearly won the war for Germany.

'The United States and Nazi Germany had enjoyed secret diplomatic relations before the war,' Swartz continues. 'Both countries shared a mutual hatred of Communist Russia and together conspired to stop the Soviet's influence on the world. The United States supported armies established by Hitler in the Ukraine and Eastern Europe, with the assistance of such figures as Reinhard Gehlen, who headed Nazi military intelligence on the Eastern Front. These 'revolutionary' groups used terrorist tactics to harass Soviet interests within the puppet states.'

IN BED WITH THE NAZIS

The situation becomes even more complicated however. Swartz explains that Hitler enjoyed playing 'both sides against the middle' and forged his own relationship with Stalin in the hope that America and Russia would destroy each other and leave Germany to enjoy the spoils that remained.

'However, a series of military mistakes culminating with the invasion of Russia by Germany forced Stalin to align himself with the Allies to defeat the Nazi terror. The United States, forced into the war because of Japan's attack on Pearl Harbor, had not forgotten their early friendship with the Third Reich. So, at the end of the war, the two former enemies negotiated a secret agreement to again join to fight the common enemy. Because of this secret agreement, many Nazis, including those who committed atrocities, were returned to positions of power and influence inside Germany. Unknown was the extent of Nazi recruitment by U.S. intelligence agencies and political organizations in the 1940s and 50s.'

As unbelievable as it sounds, the U.S. intelligence community did not balk at employing the same racist butchers they had waged war against only a short time before! Swartz goes on to give the details of 'Operation Paperclip.'

'Perhaps the most publicized program of Nazi recruitment,' Swartz says, 'is that of 'Operation Paperclip,' which involved the collection of Nazi rocket scientists and facilities, all of which were later incorporated into the U.S. Space Program. The several U.S. agencies employed hundreds, perhaps thousands, of Nazis, from the CIC to the CIA, and used them in covert operations overseas, as our first line of defense against communism. Others, as guilty of wartime atrocities, were brought into the United States for domestic political purposes. This aspect of the U.S.-Nazi connection is well documented, and deserves closer attention by the mainstream press.

'The U.S. Military secretly rounded up Nazi scientists and brought them to the United States. The original intention had been to merely debrief them and send them back to Germany. Nevertheless, when it realized the extent of the scientists' knowledge and expertise, the War Department decided it would be a waste to send the scientists home. Unfortunately, there was only one problem: it was illegal. U.S. law explicitly prohibited Nazi officials from immigrating to America and as many as three-quarters of the scientists in question had been dedicated members of the Nazi party.'

PLAYING WITH THE TRUTH

Next, the American president, Harry Truman, makes a major decision.

'President Harry Truman,' Swartz continues, 'was convinced that German scientists could help America's postwar efforts. President Truman agreed in September 1946 to authorize Operation Paperclip. However, Truman expressly excluded anyone found to have been a member of the Nazi party and more than a nominal participant in its activities, or an active supporter of Nazism or militarism. The War Department's Joint Intelligence Objectives Agency (JIOA) conducted background investigations of the scientists. In February 1947, JIOA Director Bosquet Wev submitted the first set of scientists' dossiers to the State and Justice Departments for review. Samauel Klaus, the State Department's representative on the JIOA board, claimed that all the scientists in this first batch were 'ardent Nazis.' Their visa requests were quickly denied.

'Wev was furious,' Swartz goes on. 'He wrote a memo warning that 'the best interests of the United States have been subjugated to the efforts to expended in beating a dead Nazi horse.' He also declared that the return of these scientists to Germany, where America's enemies could exploit them, presented a 'far greater security threat to this country than any former Nazi affiliations that they may have had or even any Nazi sympathies they may still have.'

'The War Department solved this problem by sanitizing their reports. They rewrote Operation Paperclip reports with any Nazi connections eliminated, allowing many Nazis entrance into the United States. In a 1985 expose in the ***Bulletin of the Atomic Scientists***,

Linda Hunt wrote that she had examined more than 130 reports on Operation Paperclip subjects, and every one 'had been changed to eliminate the security threat classification.' The United States government protected the former Nazi elite so they ostensibly could help counter the Soviet threat.

'However, for the next five decades, this decision loosened up Washington's tolerance for human rights abuses and a variety of other crimes in the name of anticommunism. The

consequences continue to this day, with an enduring influence of the fascist ideology in the United States and other western nations. This influence can trace its ideological lineage back to Adolph Hitler's Third Reich and the hope of eventual creation of a Fourth Reich.'

IS THERE A FOURTH REICH ALREADY?

It is at this point that Swartz proposes a somber possibility about where it all might have led.

'Rather than being the mad dreams of a sick dictator,' he writes, 'the Fourth Reich may be a secret reality today. The 'behind the closed door' agreements between the United States and the Nazi ruling elite could have created a secret government that has carried on the ideals of Hitler and his evil minions.'

Did the same scientists who were rumored to have pioneered flying saucer technology during the war bring those secrets with them to the U.S. in the postwar years? Did they continue to research and fly these exotic aircraft with American funding and support? Were we able to reach the Moon and even Mars many years before the public victories of our Space Program began in the 1960s because of classified Nazi know-how? We can only wait for time itself to answer these questions, but it is important that they be asked now.

(For more information on Operation Paperclip, Nazis, UFOs and the New World Order, see *Evil Agenda of the Secret Government* by Tim Swartz, published by Global Communications)

CHAPTER THREE
EXPLORING THE NAZI CONNECTION

Researcher and author Peter Moon is best known for a series of books he wrote in cooperation with Preston Nichols about a secret military installation located at Montauk Point, on Long Island, New York. There are many stories about the base itself, called Camp Hero, that have to do with alleged mind-control experiments conducted there that soon led to other bizarre technological feats such as time travel and mysterious 'portals' that allowed the Montauk Point personnel to travel anywhere in the universe instantaneously.

It was the whistle-blowing efforts of Preston Nichols, who only recovered his memories of being a Camp Hero operative years after the fact, that initially exposed the covert experiments in mind-control and time travel. In writer Peter Moon, Nichols found a capable ally with whom to further unveil the dark secrets being studied and the unknown powers being manipulated on a black budget and at taxpayers' expense.

There is a huge amount of information that has come forth from the collaboration of Moon and Nichols that can be found in such works as *The Montauk Project*. However, as one of many points of interest that have surfaced through their research efforts, Moon did uncover more fascinating details of the Nazis and their flying saucer technology, knowledge that has been locked away for more than half a century. [Peter Moon and Preston Nichols have collaborated on four books, *The Montauk Project*, *Montauk Revisited*, *Pyramids of Montauk*, and *Encounter in the Pleiades*. Moon also authored *The Black Sun*, a further continuation of the Montauk series, as a solo effort. All of the books are available from Sky Books.]

THE EVER CHANGING UFOs

'There's a theory,' Moon began, 'that the UFOs at Roswell or certainly other UFOs being sighted all over the planet were Nazi craft, including those that were buzzing the White House in 1952. You see, as we move forward with Ufology, the flying saucers get more sophisticated and increasingly high-tech. But it's sort of preposterous to think that the aliens would be moving along at our speed.' In other words, the technological changes that are seen to progress as UFOs are observed through the years are more likely the result of human advances in practical know-how and discoveries of the secret technologies as opposed to alien improvements in their ships' design.

THE SECRETS OF THE VRIL AND THULE

Moon next talked about the secret societies that may have been behind the Nazi flying saucers.

'That goes back to the Vril Society,' he explained. 'The Vril Society was one of two secret organizations put together by Karl Haushofer. The other was the Thule Society. They were brought into being after World War I. Karl Haushofer's whole trip was to reestablish the Aryan race and the German Empire. That's what World War I was about. They were trying to reestablish their Aryan supremacy but they were thwarted in the First World War. He was part of secret societies the likes of which we'll never know, and he was tied to the Tibetan 'Bon' religion.'

Besides just his membership in secret societies, Haushofer had another pair of aces up his sleeve.

'He had a couple of psychics or spiritualists,' Moon continued, 'that he was dealing with, and they were channeling the technology to build these flying saucers. The whole effort regarding the flying saucers was through the Vril Society. It was the more secretive and the more interesting, whereas the Thule Society was more concerned with the occult and served as a front for the Bavarian Illuminati. It was the Thule Society that went on to become involved with Hitler and bring him to power.'

RUDOLPH HESS AND THE 'TRUTH' ON FILM

If there was any one member of the Third Reich who was particularly interested in the development of flying saucers, it was Rudolph Hess, according to Moon.

'He used to lecture on them,' Moon said. 'And he was also deeply in to the occult.'

Moon said that there are rumored to exist certain films from that period in which Hess talks about the Vril Society and Hitler holds forth on the Ubermensch, which was his concept of the Superman and may have included his version of the aliens.

'I met a lady from Germany,' Moon said, 'who told me that her mother told her that Hitler had passed out while talking about the aliens. He got so passionate and passed out and they had to take him away on a stretcher.

'The one woman who would have full knowledge of the films,' Moon went on, 'is still alive, but she must be a hundred-years-old by now. Leni Riefenstahl. Leni Riefenstahl was a very close confidant of Hitler in an artistic sense. We know that some people claim otherwise, but she does not. But she says she only remembers three instances of being with Hitler because she was given electroshock and mind-controlled after the war by the French.'

Riefenstahl is best known for her acclaimed Nazi propaganda film *Triumph of the Will*. 'That was considered great filmmaking,' Moon said, 'whether you like Nazism or not. But she's very famous and still kicking.'

Any confirming testimony that Reifenstahl could provide about Nazi flying saucer technology will probably go to her grave with her.

DOWNLOADING THE BRAIN OF RUDOLPH HESS

Moon also had a story to relate about American attempts to ferret out the Nazis flying saucer technology. It begins with an infamous figure named Ewen Cameron, a psychiatrist who would eventually come to head the CIA mind control program dubbed MK-Ultra and is to this day still accused of doing brutal experiments on innocent test subjects.

It was in May of 1941, and Allen Dulles, the future head of the CIA, had an important assignment for Cameron. It seems that Rudolph Hess had made a secret trip into England in order to try and secure a peace agreement with the British before the war escalated to a level that not even the Nazis wanted. Hess was subjected to intense interrogation, which included being examined by Cameron.

'Cameron gave Hess mind-altering drugs,' Moon said. 'We do know that. After his examination, it was said that the Hess that ended up in Spandau Prison was no longer Hess.'

Not only did Cameron administer mind-altering drugs that caused extreme changes in Hess' personality, Cameron took a great deal of pleasure in the whole tortuous process.

'I met one of Cameron's protégés,' Moon said, 'and she told me that he was just really tickled over that meeting with Hess. He said that's where it all started. He was able to put mind-altering drugs into Hess and download every bit of information in him, and find out all about the Nazi saucers. Right there, you had a transfer of power from the Nazis and all of their occult and UFO lore began to drift to the Allies through the personage of Ewen Cameron.

'Again, Hess knew about the Nazi occultism and he knew about their flying saucer program because he used to lecture on it. He used to lecture prolifically on it. Whether he was giving a popular layman's lecture or one with more technological details-- he was never known as a technological person. But whatever that information was, Ewen Cameron had complete and utter access to it in 1941. It was before the Philadelphia Experiment. We would have known about it. We wouldn't have necessarily known their exact technology, but we would have known the general history and an overview of it at least.'

Not that the Nazi flying saucers were a complete success.

'They were wobbly and unstable,' Moon said, 'they were not good for fighting. The Nazis spent most of their money on conventional weapons. So these things were not what you'd call good fighting machines because they weren't honed for that purpose.'

NAZIS FROM A PARALLEL UNIVERSE

Still another rumor of Nazi otherworldly technology has come to Moon's attention. In a book written by Glenn Pruitt, the concept of Nazi control of or access to a parallel universe through the Montauk Control Center is given serious consideration.

'Its comic bookish,' Moon concedes. 'However, what he says about parallel universes is very valid in quantum physics, as far as their being an infinity of them, and if we are being controlled, it would stand to reason that parallel universes would play a role. And that they might include Nazis makes it all the more interesting and intriguing. So that's another angle to the Nazi connection. People don't like reading something comic bookish that sounds like speculation. However, in quantum physics, everything exists. Everything is a potential and a possibility.'

THE PORTAL TO MARS

Moon said that Preston Nichols, the original psychic whistleblower in the investigation of the Montauk mysteries, once told him that there was something similar to the Nazis portal into a parallel universe located at Montauk itself.

'There was a Montauk connection to Mars,' Moon said. 'They went to Mars and saw that there was an underground city on Mars. There was a time portal that went straight from Montauk to Mars. They could go anywhere they wanted to at Montauk, and that's where they went. They went to Mars and accessed something called the Solar System Defense Shield. There wasn't a whole lot of information, however.'

That lack of concrete information continues to daunt even the best efforts to learn the ultimate truth behind the many tantalizing rumors concerning flying saucer technology and early attempts by secret scientific organizations to fly to Mars. Clearly, it is a case in which what we don't know not only hurts us, it frustrates us in the extreme. For the time being, we must let the rumors and clandestinely whispered tales of Nazi flying saucers stand or fall on their own merits.

CHAPTER FOUR
OVER HALF A CENTURY ON THE MOON

Having established that the great UFO flap of 1897-97 may have been the visible manifestation of secret *human* technology, as well as the fact that the Nazis were discovered to be on the forefront of improving the nineteenth century technology to a point where it seemed like anything was possible, the next phase in the story this book will tell will boggle the mind even more.

According to several credible postings on the Internet, mankind reached the Moon and Mars many years before the conventional wisdom would have it. Perhaps these gentlemen chose to remain anonymous for the sake of their own safety in the murky world of conspiracy and intrigue. Nevertheless, they are still major contributors to our knowledge of this subject.

ON THE MOON IN 1942

The first posting begins with a headline that reads: HALF A CENTURY OF THE HUMAN MOON BASE, 1942-1992.

'The Germans landed on the Moon,' the author Vladimir Terziski begins, 'as early as probably 1942, utilizing their larger exo-atmospheric rocket saucers of the Schriever type. The Miethe rocket craft was built in diameters of 15 to 50 meters, and the Schriever-Walter turbine was designed as an interplanetary vehicle. It had a diameter of 60 meters and had 10 stories of crew compartments several meters high. Welcome to Alice in Saucerland.

'In my extensive research of dissident American theories about the physical conditions on the Moon,' the noted researcher on antigravity flight continues, 'I have proved without a shadow of a doubt that there is atmosphere, water and vegetation on the Moon, and that man does not need a spacesuit. A pair of jeans, a pullover and sneakers are just about enough. Everything NASA has told the world about the Moon is a lie and it was done to keep the exclusivity of the club from Third World countries. All these physical conditions make it a lot easier to build a Moon base. Ever since their first day on the Moon, the Germans started boring and tunneling under the surface, and by the end of the war there was a small base on the Moon.'

The author next gives some technical background on the craft used by the Nazis as well as some interesting political history.

'The Free Energy tachyon drive craft of the Haunibu-1 and B2 type were used after 1944 to haul people, material and other essentials to the construction site on the Moon,' he writes. 'When Russians and Americans secretly landed together on the Moon in the early versions of their own saucers, they spent their first night as guests of the Nazis in their underground base.

'In the 60s,' Terziski goes on, 'a massive Russian-American base had been built on the Moon that now has a population of 40,000, rumor goes. After the end of the war in 1945, the Germans continued their space effort from their south polar stronghold called 'Schwabenland.' I have discovered a photograph of their underground space control center there.'

[It would be great to see such a photograph, but as the saying goes, 'It might as well be on the Moon.']

ONE HAND WASHES THE OTHER

Section two of the posting is headlined: GERMAN-JAPANESE MILITARY R & D COOPERATION.

'According to Renato Vesco again,' Vladimir writes, 'Germany was sharing a great deal of the advances in weaponry with their allies during the war. At the Fiat experimental facility at Lake La Garda, a facility that fittingly bore the name of air marital Hermann, Italians were experimenting with numerous advanced weapons, rockets and airplanes created in Germany. In a similar fashion, Germans kept a close contact with the Japanese military establishment and were supplying it with many advanced designs.

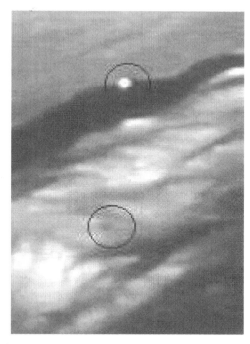

Photographs taken from both ground-based telescopes and satellites in orbit show strange artifacts that some have said are actual secret bases on the Moon.
These structures could be German or Russian/American bases constructed in secret just after World War II.

'A Japanese friend of mine in Los Angeles,' he continues, 'related to me the story of his friend's father, who worked as a technician in the intelligence bureau during the war. In July of 1945, two and a half months after the war ended in Germany, a huge submarine brought to Japan the latest of German inventions-- two spherical wingless flying devices.

'The Japanese assembled the machines together, following the German instructions, and there was something very bizarre and otherworldly about them-- a ball-shaped flying device without wings or propellers, that nobody knew how it worked. The fuel was added to the fuel tanks of this unmanned machine and it disappeared with a roar of flames into the sky. They tested the other one, and the engineers were so frightened by the unexpected might of the machine that they promptly dynamited it and chose to forget the whole incident.'

MARS OR BUST

The third and final headline offered by this source reads: GERMAN-JAPANESE FLIGHT TO MARS IN 1945-46.

'According to the authors of the underground German documentary movie from the Thule Society, the Hannibu-3 type the 74 meter diameter naval warfare dreadnought-- was chosen for the most courageous mission of the 20th Century the trip to Mars. The craft was saucer shape, had the bigger Andromeda tachyon drives, and was armed with gun turrets of large naval caliber (three inverted upside down and attached to the underside of the craft).

'A volunteer suicide crew of Germans and Japanese was chosen, because everybody knew that this journey was one from which they would not return. The large intensity of the electromagnetic fields and the inferior quality of the metal alloys used caused metal fatigue and the ship began to get very brittle after only a few months of work. The flight took off from Germany one month before the war ended in April 1945.

'It was probably a large crew,' the anonymous report continues, 'numbering in the hundreds, because of the low level of automation and electronic control of the saucer. Most of the systems of the craft had to be operated like those on a U-Boat of that time-- manually. Because the weakened tachyon drives were not working with full power and not all the time, the trip to Mars took almost eight months. An initial thrust towards Mars was probably used to take advantage of the strong gravitational field close to Earth, after which the craft began an eight-month elliptical flight to Mars with its main drives turned off.

'Later trips to Mars by the joint Soviet-American effort and by the Vatican craft of the Marconi project from Argentina in 1956 reached Mars in only two to three days, because the engines kept working through the whole flight, accelerating in the first half and decelerating in the second half. Smaller Kohler converters were used to power the systems and life support equipment on board. I do not have any information at the present time about gravity capability onboard the craft, but that could have been easily done with the large antigravity drives of the ship itself.

'After a heavy, almost crash landing, the saucer slammed to a stop, damaging irreparably its drives, but saving some members of the crew. This event happened in January 1946. The crash landing on Mars was not only due to the crippled tachyon drive but was also caused by the smaller gravitational field of Mars generating less power for the tachyon drives, and also due to the atmosphere on Mars, that could not be used as effectively for breaking as the Earth's atmosphere could.

'One question that I have not answered yet in the affirmative is how were the Germans able to regenerate the air supply for eight months for this big crew. Quite probably they were using advanced life support systems, developed initially for the turbine and free energy submarines that were cruising the oceans without resurfacing.

'The radio message,' the report concludes, 'with the mixed news of their partial success was received by the German underground space control center in NeuStadt, their research base on the Moon.'

ACTUAL BASES THAT COME SOON AFTER

Another report posted on the Internet is offered freely. It is entitled **'Bases On Mars'** and gives the relevant details of three separate bases believed to be alien controlled but employing human beings as workers in an almost slave-like condition. The notes are terse and a little fragmented, but still worthy of inclusion.

The information was posted on March 8, 1997.

'Place: North East of the planet-- there is no water to separate the continents. Built on a plateau.

'Purpose and general information: TO COORDINATE THE TAKEOVER OF EARTH

'Laser projected pictures of whatever they wish to see. From here the areas they want to keep 'clean' for their takeover are marked. This means the soils that should stay out of use. Programs naturally are originated in Andromeda and refined here. A team of experts in takeover tactics. Done many times before all over the different galaxies, whenever things get too much out of their control. In these bases, Homo Sapiens are working, hoping for a better condition for themselves and for some few others of the 'chosen ones.'

'As we have seen before, they can pinpoint the places where they want inundation to occur. They have NOTHING against us in particular, just a job that must be executed. They are used to winning, as the 'enemy' is undetected. The three bases are connected subterraneously. The Moon is used as their satellite. (Most planets have 'moons.') From Mars, some make trips to the Moon or to Earth to check on different conditions on the spot.

'Their job is INFILTRATION AND WAR. Here they have programs for each base on Earth, Mars and the Moon. Here it is played with, the value of currencies all over Earth. The intention being that the masses of population should have less, having apparently 'more.' This we came to call inflation! Economy is made to appear so complicated that everyone is kept in confusion about it. Simplicity is not taught: spend less than what you earn, and you will always have!

'Terrorism is planted with exactness, taking into consideration different places, as well as its timing. As I said before, all is aimed at ONE WORLD ORDER. All this is a tiny part of a huge Organization, and no one in it is free! This is a big enslaving machine for everyone involved. If a break appears in the system here on Earth, the whole organization will start to shatter as it is built very much the same way all over the place and there naturally is interconnection.'

BASE NUMBER ONE

'Purpose: Food and Medicine Supply.
Storage for spare parts that might be needed.

Ships arrive here and are placed in shelter as there are terrible winds that sometimes carry stones.

'Composed of: Extraterrestrials 28-Hybrids 350-Homo Sapiens about 90. These are here because they are considered of no use in any other place. Storage space is huge as there is no necessity to hide, but much is built underground for protection against the elements. For our scientists on Earth, many stops are being made when they want to 'visit' Mars, as there are obviously areas which should not be seen or studied!

'In storage there are also spare parts that are much needed on Earth, part of the reason for the lively traffic between these two planets. Possibly astronomers could spot this? Here we have really big INTERGALACTIC ships. As mentioned before, enough space without fear of detection. These ships come and go. Sometimes there can be three of them in the area.

'Food supplies come from Earth. There is underground water in the area!

'Twenty own ships. (For them to come to Earth is like for someone from the U.S. to fly to Paris!) There is also here some stock of live animals that reproduce themselves. 'Green Gardens,' all under one roof. Very much as in science-fiction.

'A hospital, naturally, only equipped with their advanced technology. It includes a psychiatric ward where implants are perpetrated for missions as well as to subdue ANY revolt.

'All is very peaceful in these bases. Sex is not allowed in any of the three bases. Only grownups are admitted. Age 20 as minimum. Anyone that is of no use to them gets eliminated by implanting the being to be used against us 'down here.' Due to this system, all work as efficiently as they can. Fear drives them, not ideals! Possibly this is the reason that I am allowed to come out with this data. They want us to KNOW about their situation!'

One can see the obvious strain this anonymous author is under as he writes this. Perhaps he really has been through the mill with aliens on Mars!

BASE NUMBER TWO

'Purpose: To Coordinate the Programs They Have With The Actual Situations.

'The purpose is settled, but to be able to achieve it they have to be somewhat flexible. As we already know from the bases on Earth, they gather information from all over the place. The main information comes here, where, with a clear view of the WHOLE planet's situation, programs are prepared or changed as needed. Each one is made for a specific base. Whatever activity is done from a base on the Moon, the orders come from this 'Base Number Two.' (The base on the Moon is situated on the backside of it. Just 'around the corner,' not to be seen from Earth.)

'Composed of: Extraterrestrials 400-Hybrids 3,000-Homo Sapiens 500. Homo Sapiens is needed to evaluate certain situations. Space for computers. Space for picture projections.

Space for analysis. Conference rooms. Space for telepathic communications. Space for relaxing. All very spacious! The 'amazing' thing is that they have very little discussions or disagreements. Basically, all are prisoners in different degrees.'

BASE NUMBER THREE

'Purpose: Sending Out Orders That Should Be Executed.

'There is more movement in this base. Most is done by their Internet system, through which they can talk and be seen as well as transmit written materials. Sometimes people are brought up here to be instructed or trained, or implanted to ensure execution. Other times some leave from here to give instructions to people on bases on Earth or the Moon. One could say that they can work with the 'speed of light.'

'This being the fastest moving organization in the area. The reason for this is that if a change of plans has to be done, not to lose their power, it has to be done fast!

'Composed of: The fastest brains in terms of ACTION. 350 Grays-300 Hybrids-75 Homo Sapiens. Under the command of this base there is a crew for handling their ships. Only the best ones are stationed here. Sixty hybrid pilots, as they are more dispensable. No Homo Sapiens as pilots are allowed, as they are afraid they might escape.

'Post Scripture: Amazing, but all wish to be able to be free to decide on what they want to do, and the way to do it. UNTIL NOW THIS HAS BEEN UNATTAINABLE. Strange as it may sound, through this message they are seeking help!'

PUTTING TWO AND TWO TOGETHER

While it is apparent that these two anonymous reports don't jibe together perfectly, one can still sort of begin to assemble a composite picture or logical storyline. It would go like this: The Nazis, and later America, Russia, and even the Vatican, had the capability, at some point in the 1940s and 50s, to put human beings on the Moon and Mars. Perhaps they had a nudge in the right direction technologically from the aliens, who had their own purposes for wanting mankind to move into outer space.

Then, having arrived at their destination, the human space travelers became enmeshed in the aliens' agenda, becoming little more than slave labor, imprisoned both physically and psychologically. The aliens' agenda would then likely read like just another variation on the standard New World Order conspiracy theories.

Agreed, the total picture remains a little hazy here, but complete clarity on this subject may be coming sooner than we dare imagine!

CHAPTER FIVE
FRANK ZNIDARSIC'S SEARCH
FOR "FREE ENERGY"

If the seemingly miraculous aircraft technology described in the previous chapters actually worked, it must have done so with some form of Free Energy still unknown to us, the general public. Solid rocket fuel or other known propulsion methods simply could not have achieved the alleged success of the legendary manmade UFOs.

Frank Znidarsic is an unsung hero of the battle to create Free Energy in our present time. In the following interview conducted for this book, Znidarsic discusses some of the promising work being done in the field, as well as giving his opinions on the pioneering work of Nikola Tesla and offering his thoughts about the possibility of manmade UFOs appearing on the horizon soon.

FIRST THINGS FIRST

Question: I'd like to start off by asking you for some biographical background on yourself.

Znidarsic: Okay. I'm an electrical engineer. I graduated from the University of Pittsburgh at Johnstown. I'm a registered professional engineer in the state of Pennsylvania. I also have a business degree from St. Francis University, and I completed a core course in physics and computer science at Indiana University. And I've been working in the power generating industry for 23 years.

Question: So how did you get interested in these futuristic technologies?

Znidarsic: Well, that's sort of the story that I wanted to tell you. Back in the 1980s, I was involved in power generation and mining, and I saw the environmental damage and I also saw that the fuels were limited. And I was looking for new forms of energy. Initially, I got involved with solar energy and renewables, and I had great hope that that was going to be the wave of the future, as it was pretty much touted at that period. However, my studies revealed that it never really would supplement fossil fuels, that it could provide supplemental power in certain applications. But to really drive society and move people ahead and provide things to increase our standard or living, I didn't think it was going to do it.

SOMETHING FROM NOTHING

At that point I began to think of radically different methods of power generation. And what I thought of was quite different, and what I thought of was, I knew the principle of the conservation of energy, that energy is neither created nor destroyed. So you have to have something, like burning oil to produce electricity and then convert the electricity to heat. You always have something converted into something else.

But I wondered how the universe started, the initial event. We have all this material in our wonderful universe, and we know from the Big Bang Theory that 15 billion years ago it started from nothing. And I wondered, here was something-- everything that was created from nothing can we understand this process? And can we make energy by the same process that the universe itself was created with?

And that proved to be a very, very difficult project, until I read about the work of Dr. Edward Trion, at Hunter City College. He's very famous. What he said was the universe is a 'vacuum fluctuation,' which means the total energy of the universe is zero. For instance, the positive energy of everything we observe is balanced by negative gravitational potential. So if you have an object, it has positive energy in it. But this object also has gravity associated with it, and that gravity reaches out toward the entire universe. And the universe itself then falls a little deeper into a hole. So we're in a gravitational hole. The entire universe is.

And the amount of energy in the universe is equal to the depth of the hole. Now a good example would be if you had a rocket ship, a **perfectly** efficient rocket ship, and it was climbing and climbing up higher and higher in the sky and consumed its fuel. This rocket ship was a hundred percent efficient, so it started consuming the furniture and the structure. It started consuming itself as it goes higher and expends more fuel. And finally, when it reaches the edge of the universe, the rocket ship consumes everything. There's nothing left. It took everything that that ship had to reach the edge of the universe. Likewise, if you could start from nothing at the edge of the universe and fall in, you could produce a rocket ship, materials, energy, by the reverse process.

CONTROLLING GRAVITY

And then I fundamentally realized that in order to do this, you had to be able to control gravity in order to produce energy. And it was a real problem with controlling gravity. Nobody really knew how to do it. We understand gravity, but there's something called the

Constants of the Motions that are wrong. For instance, an electrical generator, you can make a very strong field in a generator and make electricity, and the device can fit in a building. But in order to produce usable gravity, you have to have an object as large as the Earth moving around. So obviously we can't build a piece of equipment as large as the Earth to make gravity do what we want to do. So it would be very, very impractical.

WHAT IS COLD FUSION?

And then about 1989, Pons and Fleischmann announced that they discovered this remarkable cold fusion. And many people like Robert Parks and Peter Zimmerman said, 'Oh, you can't have fusion in a bottle because it requires temperatures greater than the interior of the sun.' And yet they continued to demonstrate anomalous energy. And this guy James Patterson invented his Patterson Power Cell. Motorola offered him $60 million, but he couldn't always get it to work. And finally one of my best friends and a leader in this field is Dr. George Miley at the University of Illinois, and he's had these cold fusion cells working.

What I observed when I went there is that the ones that work are made of little tiny structures, fifty nanometers in diameter. And I thought, 'That size has to be important.' And then I noticed that the vibrations, the thermal vibrations, were like 10 to 13 hertz, the vibrations associated with thermal energy. The product, multiply the size, the fifty nanometers diameter times the 10 to the 13th hertz, and the result is one megahertz meter. I thought, 'That has to be important for something.'

Question: Okay, that's very technical stuff. Could you break that down a little bit?

Znidarsic: Yeah. The size of the particles is important in order to produce the cold fusion.

Question: Right. What is cold fusion? I don't even know what that is, I'm afraid.

Znidarsic: Cold fusion is an energy source that seems to produce energy by nuclear reactions. But there's no radiation. Also, it's not composed of uranium or anything to produce nuclear reactions. And it's much too cold to produce power by the same process as a nuclear bomb.

Question: Is it like splitting the atom in some kind of cold environment?

Znidarsic: Well, there are a lot of things that happen. Professor Miley found that not only do you split atoms, but you also produce heavy elements. One element changes into silver. It's a really, really strange, unknown phenomenon.

Question: You mean you can create silver like an alchemist?

Znidarsic: Yes, but very tiny amounts.

On March 23, 1989, Stanley Pons and Martin Fleischmann announced their discovery of cold fusion, the production of usable amounts of energy by a nuclear process occurring in a jar of water at room temperature.

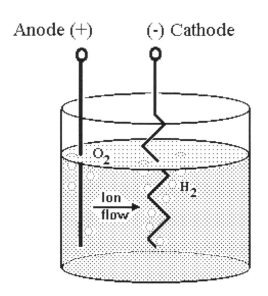

The cathode is palladium in a typical heavy water cell and nickel in a typical light water cell. The CETI cell contains layers of nickel palladuim and copper.

The electrolyte is light or heavy water and a salt. The salt is usually lithium sulfate.

A TYPICAL COLD FUSION CELL

Illustration courtesy of Frank Znidarsic -
www.angelfire.com/scifi2/zpt/index.html

BLOWING SMOKE

Anyway, about 1992 or 93, [a scientist named] Eugene Podkletnov was spinning a super-conductive disc and he hit it with a radio wave. He was doing some odd experiments. And a friend came in smoking a pipe, and right about the center of the super-conductive disc, the smoke rose. And they said, 'Wow, that's really, really strange.' They went into the room above it and they blew smoke and they noticed the same phenomenon penetrated the floor.

And then Podkletnov discovered a gravitational anomaly that got a lot of people quite excited, including NASA-Marshall. And I was down to visit NASA at their invitation and met with Lott Bradley, the director of the advanced concepts office, and they're trying to reproduce this effect. They really expect to have some results within a year or so. Then what I noticed was, the disc was one third of a meter in diameter, and they were hitting it with three megahertz radio waves. And I got the diameter of the disc and the frequency again, one third of a meter times three megahertz was one megahertz meter. It was the same constant that Miley had in his cold fusion cell, however it was producing a gravitational anomaly, not a thermal anomaly.

ZNIDARSIC'S THEOREM

And then I put this together with my own work, and I came up with this theorem. And I'll say this very precisely. And it is: the gravitational and electrical motion constants tend toward those of the electromagnetic in the Bose condensate that stimulated a dimensional frequency of one megahertz meter. That's a technical thing, and a mouthful.

And what does that mean? Well, there are three states of matter, solid, liquid and gas, that most people are familiar with. A lot of inventors have worked with all three states, and they're never going to get any extra energy. But there's another state of matter. It's called Bose condensate. Now Bose condensate is really, really strange. It's what a super-conductor is made of. You put electrical current in it and it flows forever. There are also liquid forms of it. Liquid helium is a Bose condensate. You spin it in a jar and it spins forever. It never stops. These are all known phenomena. So this is really a different, altered state of matter.

And they're finding out new things about it all the time. It's not really completely understood. But there were never any nuclear or gravitational anomalies associated with the Bose condensate. So what I discovered is if you stimulate, vibrate this Bose condensate at the right frequency, you can get gravitational and nuclear anomalies. And that's what Podkletnov did when he hit this super-conductive disc, one-third of a meter diameter, with three megahertz radio waves. And that's what Miley did when he heated up the 50 nanometer parts of his cold fusion cells.

WHERE DOES THIS LEAD?

Now what does this really mean? What's coming? Well, all of the technology that we see today is based on the control of the electromagnetic field. For instance, the television, the computer, transistors, communications. We can control the electromagnetic field that was originally discovered by Faraday.

But there are also other forces in the universe. There's a gravitational force and a nuclear force. But we've never been able to control them. One of the reasons is because gravity has the wrong motion constant, which means it takes an object as large as the entire Earth to produce a field. Nuclear forces, we haven't been able to control them because it has such a short range. That means it also has the wrong motion constants. If we built a machine, it would have to be as small as the nucleus of an atom to really interact. So they've been out of the realm of possibility.

But now that we understand it, we can change this motion constant thing, which means we may be able to control the gravitational force and the nuclear force in the same manner that we control electricity. That doesn't mean it's going to unify or become one. That means we're going to be able to control them. And the host of technologies that could emerge from that could be enormous. It could be three times what we see today. But everything we see today is controlled by an electromagnetic field. If we learn how to control other fields, we should have three times the technology.

Now what these technologies are I can't even envision them all. But I can tell you what I see is energy production, propulsion, and nuclear waste reduction, a neutralization of the nuclear waste. And I think the possibilities go on. We're at a very early and fundamental stage. Of course there are a lot of people who have a lot of different theories, but I think I'm correct. I think I've contributed significantly to the ongoing effort.

SOME HELPFUL CLARIFICATION

Question: You mentioned two different kinds of anomalies. One was a gravitational one. When you say anomaly, you mean something out of the ordinary?

Znidarsic: Out of the ordinary. For instance, like any kind of matter will produce a gravitational field, but it would be so tiny we'd never detect it. You need a whole pile as big as the Earth. But this super-conductive disc produced a weight reduction of about one or two percent, and the disc was only something you could put in your hand.

Question: So essentially what 'gravitational anomaly' meant was that you could reduce the weight of an object.

Znidarsic: Above it. Right.

Question: And you also mentioned another kind of anomaly. What was that?

Znidarsic: A thermal anomaly. Cold fusion.

Question: You make something cold or hot then?

Znidarsic: Hot. It makes something hot. It doesn't make a lot of energy, but they kept it going for days and days, and they figured if it was made out of fuels or anything, it should have burned itself up. The energy produced by this cold fusion reaction was beyond chemicals.

Question: You created a form of heat then without having to burn any fuel to do it.

Znidarsic: Right. It's a very small amount of heat and it's very difficult. The cell costs about $20,000 to build right now. It's not practical, but it's there.

Question: So these are both concepts that are labeled as 'Free Energy'? Am I correct in using that term?

Znidarsic: Well, they're not free. One depends on changing nuclear states. That's the cold fusion. And another one depends on; but effectively they would be free because once you built and got the cost down on the cell, it would continue to produce energy.

ZNIDARSIC ON TESLA

Question: What do you have to say about Nikola Tesla?

Znidarsic: I'm very interested in one thing that Nikola Tesla did, and that is to make artificial balls of lightning. Lighting makes a streak and then it goes out in like a millisecond. Sometimes a little ball forms. And one time these little balls went into a tub and they heated the whole tub to boiling. The question is, how did this thing continue to glow after it's disconnected from the electrical circuit? Some anomalous energy must be involved. I think it's closely related to cold fusion but I really haven't been able to put my finger on it. Other than that the most recent tests have indicated that they found dust around the ball of lighting and the size of the dust was 50 nanometers.

It's the same size as the particles in the cold fusion cell. So we don't know, but if ball lighting could be produced artificially, it may be usable as an energy source.

Question: Do you think Nikola Tesla is an important figure historically? Does he have credibility with you?

Znidarsic: Oh, yes. Nikola Tesla has credibility. He developed a lot of the stuff that is associated with AC power that you have in your house. Transformers, generators. Thomas Edison believed in Direct Current, and Nikola Tesla believed in the AC. And

George Westinghouse sort of bought his patent, and that's how the Westinghouse Corporation started and that's how we began to electrify America.

But what I don't believe about Nikola Tesla is that his ideas were beyond that. I mean, they were great and they changed our society, but I don't believe he was light years beyond where we are today. He saw very far from where he was at, but I don't believe he had remarkable machines that we still haven't developed.

But I'm very interested in how he claimed to be able to make artificial balls of lighting. I would like to know more about that. That's something that we can't do, and it was said that he did.

Question: One of the legends about Tesla was that he designed a machine that could detect storms from a distance, from hundreds of miles away. He created some kind of weather detection device and he began to hear alien voices speaking to him through it. Is that the sort of stuff you think is not too believable?

Znidarsic: That's pretty far out. Because we have very, very good receivers now, with tubes and transistors and satellite systems. It's much more advanced than he had. And if heard them, we should hear them very strongly now.

MORE FUTURE POSSIBILITIES

Question: What are some of the other fantastic possibilities for future technology that you've discovered? I notice on your web site you have a chapter devoted to levitation, for instance.

Znidarsic: See, that's the gravitational stuff with the super-conducting disc. One thing I would like to say, though, is there's a lot of people out there who have inventions to make energy, and they make claims and they never quite produce. And what I'm talking about is people like Podkletnov and Miley, and other people who I think really have credible devices. And they're really honest and hardworking, but are just not quite there yet. There are things that are happening that have the possibility of changing everything.

Question: Well, please, talk about some of the stuff that's out there if you would.

Znidarsic: Well, this cold fusion thing. I was at Powergen in Anaheim, California, and a guy named James Patterson-- it was on the NBC Nightly News and everything. He produced this cell that made 1000 watts of energy, and Motorola offered him $60 million for it, because they tested it in their lab. And I was very excited. I thought it was just around the corner. And then he had problems with his materials. The thing didn't last very long. Then he had problems with replication. The next time he tried to build the device, it didn't work quite right. There was some kind of contaminate in very small portions in his materials that made the thing work or not work.

And that was picked up by the University of Illinois' Professor Miley. And he's continuing to test that and he's demonstrated some power, but very small amounts.

Also, along with that, is Edmond Storm, a retired scientist in Los Alamos. I went out to visit him, and he has the same kind of cell that produces this energy. Also, at the Naval Weapons lab, Scott Albert Chubak, has announced that they've also demonstrated this energy. And I'm thinking, well, considering we're up against global warming, we're running out of fuel, we're getting into wars over energy, jeeze, we need to spend more money and develop this. However, it's so unbelievable that a lot of the current scientific establishment pooh-poohs it. And they really can't get the money to move ahead the way they should be.

Dr. Edmond Storms (right) Director of ENECO meets Frank Znidarsic (left). ENECO of Salt Lake City holds the rights to the Pons and Fleishmann technology. Znidarsic was the first to identify that the palladium-deuterium electrochemical cell

(seen at center) is a room temperature super conductor.

Question: I remember reading online recently that there are these scientists in Australia who think they've got the beginnings of a teleportation machine. Have you heard about that?

Znidarsic: Yes, I have. I really don't understand everything about that, but they're able to change a bit of information between one point and another. That's as far as it went. It's going to be a long race before they can teleport anything. It's a strange universe. There are possibilities that go beyond common sense.

I also read about a lot of people producing energy machines that work with a gas or a liquid or matter or some kind of material, and I don't believe in any of that because it's going to take something more. And what it does take is a new form of matter called a Bose condensate, which is different. It's where the electrons condense like water condenses on a windshield. The electrons similarly condense and it's actually not a liquid, solid or gas, but a thing of its own. That's kind of the stuff we have to look at in order to develop exotic technology.

THE POTENTIAL OF THE UNIVERSE

Question: Well, another concept that I wanted to discuss with you, this again comes from the Tesla material-- he basically felt that the universe consists of energy. Reality all around us consists of varying degrees of energy. And would it be possible somehow to tap into that energy? Bypass fuels and generators and stuff.

Znidarsic: Right, right. Exactly. Just imagine this for a second now. You're sitting on the top of a hill with your car and you coast down the hill. As you coast down to the bottom of the hill you can charge your battery. And the energy that you've gained when you go down the hill produces power. Gravity pulls you down the hill.

Let's take the opposite scenario. Suppose you had a machine that could make gravity. And that gravity weight reaches out so it would hit the Moon. The Moon would fall a little bit. The sun would fall. You would hit a billion stars in a billion galaxies, and each would fall a little bit. That falling motion would come out as energy in your equipment. You'd be able to tap into the potential of the entire universe if you could make a machine that made gravity. And that's what Podkletnov is doing. He's showing us how. It has tremendous energy implications.

REJECTED BY MAINSTREAM SCIENCE

Question: Why do you think mainstream science so vehemently rejects this kind of research? Do you think they're afraid of something?

Znidarsic: Well, they have their paradigms. They're not really afraid. A lot of them haven't taken the time to look into it. Another thing; there are a lot of crackpots out there with a lot of crackpot ideas. And they don't have time to look at each crackpot thing that's out there. I don't consider myself a crackpot even though I do consider myself to be one who 'thinks outside the box.' Mainstream scientists are beginning to look at cold fusion. The Naval Weapons Lab has come out with a report that says they've got something, and that's right on the Net.

The problem is nobody's taking it seriously enough to be funding it. Peter Zimmerman at the State Department, he raises a stink if the government begins funding it, saying it's a waste of taxpayers money. And people's reputations are on the line.

But what I do-- science is based on rules, like rules of law. And one of them being you can't go over the speed limit. But these rules in science are called Conservation Laws. One is that energy can be neither created nor destroyed. And I looked at these newer technologies with the Conservation Laws in mind, and I find they don't violate the Conservation Laws. They are possible, although difficult.

But another scientist or an inventor who may not even be aware of them may have an idea that directly violates one of these rules, and it will never work.

Question: Well, you know, you hear these rumors sometimes of someone who actually invents a form of energy that is not dependent on fossil fuels, and then they quietly disappear.

Znidarsic: Mostly because it doesn't work. I've never come across discrimination or being put under the table. I've found people willing to look at my stuff. As a matter of fact, Los Alamos invited to come out so they could look at some of the stuff I had and they had their people test it. I've never found any problem. If you have something and you can demonstrate it, there are organizations that will look at it. They won't fund you, but they'll look at it.

TOO MUCH OF NOTHING

Question: One of the things you were trying to explain to me is that, just as the universe was created out of nothing, we should be able to create a form of energy.

Znidarsic: Out of the same process. What the Catholic Church has said is that man is able to change from one thing to another. But the universe was created by God, ex nihilio. This is what Thomas Aquinas said. That to create something from nothing was something only God could do. Man could not. Man could take what God created and change it. As we're coming to understand this creation process, I believe that we can actually do the same thing ourselves. In that same kind of process through which the universe formed, create something from nothing. And that would be the energy. In order to do that, we have to control gravity.

I think it's a very interesting idea and that it is very possible. It happened once, it could happen again. How do we do it? And can we do it?

Question: I understand you have accomplished something very important in the field.

Znidarsic: My accomplishment was taking the work of the cold fusion people, taking the work of the gravitational people, understanding what it meant, and coming up with the theorem that the gravitational and nuclear motion constants tend toward the electromagnetic in a Bose condensate that stimulated a dimensional frequency of one megahertz meter. What this means is, if we vibrate a super-conductor at the right frequency, that we should be able to control gravity and we should be able to control the electromagnetic field. It's sort of a basic fundamental theorem that says this is what you've got to do. And once we understand and develop that technology, we can start making generators that will make gravity to lift saucers in the air and generators that will reduce nuclear waste and devices that will seemingly produce energy apparently from nothing.

Because what that will do, it will enable us to control gravity, the strong nuclear force and the electromagnetic force. If you realize what that means, everything that you have around you, all the technology, is based on control of one force, electromagnetism. We cannot control gravity. We don't have any idea, and we can do things with the nuclear force, like make some bombs, but we really can't control it like we do with transistors and tubes and route it and vector it and make it do for us what we want it to do. But this idea should enable us to do that. It could greatly increase the possibilities of where our society can go.

A QUESTION OF RIDICULE

Question: How many years down the line do you see that happening?

Znidarsic: It's been a very tortuous kind of path. My publications have only been in some side journals. I'm not that well known. Professor Miley has been ridiculed. He's a very competent scientist in his work. NASA-Marshall and their Advanced Concepts Office has taken a severe beating from Peter Zimmerman and also from Robert Parks, that they're wasting taxpayers money doing this venturesome research. People have to sort of duck and hide and do it in secret. And I think it's sad. We do need to do research on these kinds of things to stay ahead, to be the number one country in the world.

The budgets are very, very tiny. I'm working at a power plant right now putting some air pollution devices on. It's $300 million dollars just to treat the pollution from one cold fire power plant. That exceeds the entire national budget by hundreds of millions of dollars that are spent on this research. We really need to devote some funding there to continue along and develop what I think would be tremendous new possibilities.

MANMADE UFOs?

Question: I have interviewed Robert Park in the past. He's also a debunker of UFOs. I know what it's like to deal with that guy.

Znidarsic: I don't know if there are UFOs or not. I've never seen one. It's possible, but whether or not they're there, I don't know. But this process they're working on, this Eugene Podkletnov, spinning super-conductive discs, and the experiments to duplicate it at NASA-Marshall, will lead to a manmade UFO. And that could get us into space very cheaply if we can get it working.

Question: There are some conspiracy theorists that think we already have done that. We already have the technology to fly a UFO and so forth. Some people feel that the entire UFO phenomenon started with Nazi scientists during the war.

Znidarsic: Possibly. But I know what I've done. I'm the guy who's developing some of the theories to make this work. I've never read it in any books, it's never been anywhere I've seen. If they're doing it, they're pretty well classified. And I'm getting the fundamental ideas of just how can we make this happen? I think we've got to get to that point before we can move ahead.

Question: Well, have you heard this kind of stuff before, that German scientists during the war developed all kinds of amazing, futuristic technologies and so forth?

Znidarsic: Yes, I have. I know they developed the jet plane and the V-2 rocket, which were quite ahead of their time. In the nuclear field, they were way behind on the bomb compared to where we were in nuclear technology.

Question: The whole Werner Von Braun and Operation Paperclip-

Znidarsic: Well, how much can you expect from a people at war when they're getting bombed? This stuff is hard to do. I would say they were limited. They developed a lot of remarkable technology, considering the constraints they were under, but I think it is really going to take a free society with money and time for people to sort through these ideas and come up with the answers. They were really under the gun, and I don't they could have done as much as people claimed.

Question: There are people who believe we were on the Moon in the 1950s, and that we've got people on Mars even as we speak.

Znidarsic: Well, rockets are very hard and very big and it costs millions of dollars to get them up there. If you did something like that, it would be known. The government would notice it. If we're living in a world of lies-- I don't think so. It might be, but in my opinion the chance is very slim. But the possibility exists that we could get there real soon if the people who have the right technologies get the funding to move ahead.

NO GOOD DEED GOES UNPUNISHED

Question: Is there anything you wish to add? Some kind of final comment you'd like to make?

Znidarsic: Well, I'm trying very hard, and it's been discouraging for me. I worked for General Public Utilities Corporation and they frowned on this kind of work. I was very disappointed. And when the downsizing came, I was downsized and I felt maybe it was due to my efforts in alternate energy. I didn't really get the support that I thought I would. A lot of scientists like Bob Park have been openly critical, and I'm not a bumpkin. I had about eight years of college. But I don't know everything, of course.

I also found another group [of scientists] that is very open-minded and excited, but it doesn't work the way I thought it would. I thought if you could demonstrate something with energy, money would come flowing. What you have to do in our society is bring a product to the market and then sell it. But if it's not to the marketable stage, there isn't much money for it, even if it's fantastic. It's been a tough road. It hasn't been as easy as you might think.

Nikola Tesla in a staged publicity photo with his magnifying transmitter capable of producing millions of volts of electricity.

CHAPTER SIX
THE MYSTERIOUS NIKOLA TESLA

"The time has come," the Walrus said, "to talk of many things. Of shoes and SHIPS and sealing wax, of cabbages and kings." (Lewis Carrol, Alice in Wonderland) And, we might add, Nikola Tesla and Mars, which is the real heart of the matter where this book is concerned.

In the following interview, journalist and author Tim Swartz does indeed talk of many things, giving fascinating details of a story that, if proven to be true, would shake the world to its very foundations. Did Tesla actually work in concert with a secret society that succeeded in reaching Mars years before World War II? Swartz manages to grapple with such questions while keeping both feet on the ground, no pun intended. But first let's look at the background of both Swartz and the genius/inventor who so enthralls him, Nikola Tesla.

SOME OF SWARTZ'S PERSONAL HISTORY

Question: Let's start with some background on yourself.

Swartz: Sure. I suppose that my background actually is in television. I've been involved in television production and news since the late 1970s. As soon as I got out of college, I went right into television and remained, working at various stations as a journalist, a producer, a photographer. I've also had an interest in parapsychology, UFOs, just about anything weird and Fortean, since I was kid. And I've continued that interest now using what I've learned as a journalist in my research and investigations, to try to have a well-rounded viewpoint on these diverse subjects. As you well know, when people ask you what you do or what your interests are, if you mention that you're interested in UFOs or parapsychology, you're almost immediately branded as a hardcore believer. And that's not what I am. I look closely for evidence and verification B and you would be amazed at what you can find out by just going out and doing a little digging so to speak.

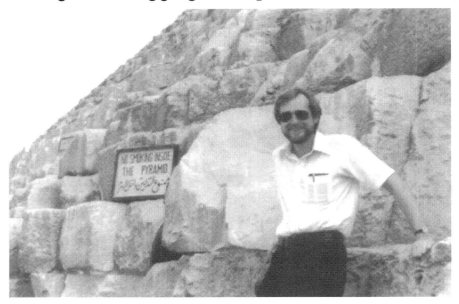

ABOVE: Television producer and author Tim Swartz has traveled the world investigating strange phenomena.

BELOW: Cult bestseller *The Lost Journals of Nikola Tesla*,

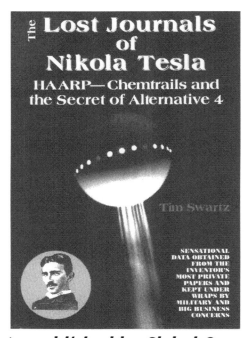

by Tim Swartz, published by Global Communications.

Question: Well, talk about your credits as a writer if you would.

Swartz: I've been a writer for Global Communications since probably around 1995. And I've written a number of books for them including my two most recent ones, *The Lost Journals Of Nikola Tesla* and then *Teleportation: From Star Trek To Tesla*, but I also have several other books that I've written for Global, like the one on time travel and books like that. But even before that I was writing magazine articles for magazines like *UFO Universe* and *UFO Sightings*. *Strange Magazine*. A magazine out of Canada called *Shadowmag*. And even as far back as *UFOlogy* and magazines like that from the 1970s. So I've been writing on these subjects for quite a while now, more than 20 years.

Actually I've been researching UFOs and paranormal phenomena since I was in high school and even before. But I mean how much can you really do until you have a car and can actually get places. So it wasn't until after I graduated from high school in 1976 that I really got serious in my research and investigations. When I could, I'd go out into the field and investigate various claims on things such as UFO sightings, poltergeist activity, Bigfoot reports etc. It's hard to believe, but the Midwest has a lot of weirdness like that. It doesn't seem to be limited to any location. So California or the East Coast can't claim all the fun.

THE SECRET LIFE OF NIKOLA TESLA

Question: Well, let's go on and talk about Nikola Tesla then. Can you give me a history of Nikola Tesla?

Swartz: Nikola Tesla was born in 1856 in what is now Yugoslavia. He passed away in 1943. So we're not talking about somebody who is alive today, but our modern electronic technology is based almost entirely upon his genius. And it's amazing to think that here we are into the 21st Century, and we are still using technology that was created by Tesla at the end of the 19th Century and the early beginnings of the 20th Century. So we have a man who was truly a super-genius along with such great minds as Leonardo da Vinci and Sir Isaac Newton. And probably the main thing that most people may not realize is that Tesla actually invented the AC motor in which our entire modern electrical system is based. Go into your kitchen. Turn on the light that comes from the great mind of Tesla. AC current. That is probably the number one thing that he is best known for. And because of that and literally hundreds of other inventions, we can enjoy our pleasant, modern way of life. Radio, remote control, robotics, X-rays, fluorescent lights, neon lights, the speedometer, the automobile ignition system, and the basics behind radar, the electron microscope, the microwave oven etc. can all be traced back to this one incredible man : Nikola Tesla.

THE BATTLE WITH THOMAS EDISON

Question: Well, why is there still so much unknown about Tesla? Why are there still all these gray areas that are so mysterious that we just haven't figured out yet?

Swartz: That's one of the sad things about the life of Tesla. Even though he was such a great genius, and contributed so much to our scientific knowledge, not that much is really remembered about this man today. A lot of it has to do with the fact that he was an eccentric personality. There's no denying that he was his own man and did things his way. And he wasn't a great businessman, like say Thomas Edison. And in fact Edison and Tesla were contemporaries and butted heads often when it came to their theories and inventions.

When Tesla first came to the United States, he started working for the Edison Company in New York. In 1887 direct current (DC) was king. At that time there were 121 Edison power stations scattered across the United States delivering DC electricity to its customers. Naturally Edison was a very big promoter of his DC current system. Unfortunately, DC current can only travel about a mile before the electricity began to lose power, while high-voltage alternating current (AC) could carry electricity hundreds of miles with little loss of power. So Tesla thought that Edison's system could use improvement and said that he had a better way. Of course Edison had a lot of money invested into his DC current, and he wasn't going to let some upstart from Europe come in and tell him that his electrical system was poorly designed.

So that right there started what would become literally years of animosity between the two. And because of that battle of the minds, Edison eventually won out in the publicity game and has actually been credited for a number of inventions that came from Tesla. If you ask most people today who invented electricity, which actually means who invented our electrical system, people will say Thomas Edison when it was actually Tesla. And Edison made sure that Tesla, whenever possible, never received the type of credit that he deserved.

And of course Tesla was his own worst enemy in that he wasn't a very good businessman, he was an idea man, and didn't handle his money well. He was constantly in debt and looking for backers to finance his projects. Because of this, he ended up losing the rights to a number of his inventions after the original patent expired. So despite all of his contributions to society, Tesla actually ended up dying almost penniless. Penniless and alone. A shade of his former self who was considered by most to be an out-of-date crackpot who talked of death-rays and free energy for all.

BIG OIL IN CONTROL

There's one school of thought that says that Tesla was a victim of a vast conspiracy by entrepreneurs such as Edison, who saw a threat in Tesla's thinking and in his inventions. It was thought that Tesla's ideas about Free Energy would take money away from those who were getting rich from the embryonic energy system. It is strikingly similar to some conspiracy theories that are circulating today concerning Big Oil and the use of and development of Free Energy devices.

The theory goes that you have these big companies who literally control the world with Big Oil and the vast profits it generates. With that kind of money and power, a Free Energy device, say something that you could just put right into your home and draw energy right from the air, would be considered a huge threat to those who have the money.

Tesla was such a genius and so far ahead of his time that even today there are engineers who try to patent what they think is an original idea only to find that it has already been patented years before by Tesla. This is why there is such a fascination with Tesla. He was coming up with ideas that seemed utter madness in the early 20th century. But now, his ideas and inventions are being looked at in a whole new light. And what is truly amazing is that most people know almost nothing about this guy. Publicity really does make a person. Edison was a shameless promoter, while Tesla wasn't. It is as simple as that.

TESLA AND FREE ENERGY

Question: Well, let's talk about Free Energy a little. What did Tesla come up with that might have led to Free Energy?

Swartz: Tesla had a number of ideas concerning Free Energy. Now, at the time, Free Energy was a term that was used for any kind of energy production that didn't involve burning something, which at the time was mostly coal. So in Tesla's day, using wind, solar energy, things like that, were considered Free Energy. Now Tesla had an idea that he could build a device that could send electrical energy around the world between the surface of the Earth and the ionosphere at extreme low frequencies in what is known as the Schumann Cavity. Knowing that a resonant cavity can be excited and that power can be delivered to that cavity it should be possible to resonate and deliver power via the Schumann Cavity to any point on Earth. This would result in practical wireless transmission of electrical power Tesla calculated in 1899 that the resonant frequency of this area was approximately 8-hertz. It was not until the 1950s that this idea was taken seriously and researchers were surprised to discover that the resonant frequency of this space was indeed in the range of 8-hertz.

Tesla also discovered in his experiments at Colorado Springs that the earth was 'literally alive with electrical vibrations.' Tesla came to think that when lightning struck the ground it set up powerful waves that moved from one side of the earth to the other. If the earth was indeed a great conductor, Tesla hypothesized that he could transmit unlimited amounts of power to any place on earth with virtually no loss. A third approach for wireless power transmission was to transmit electrical power to the area 80-kilometers above the earth known as the ionosphere. Tesla speculated that this region of the atmosphere would be highly conductive and again his suspicions were correct.

So this kind of thinking probably riled some of his backers who were getting rich off of the electrical generating system that Tesla had developed at Niagara Falls. His backers, who were looking at the potential of almost unlimited wealth coming off of this power system were not about to let him develop another competitive system.

Now Tesla also had other ideas about Free Energy where he actually patented a device for the "Utilization of Radiant Energy." Tesla used the vernacular of his day and said it would collect "Cosmic Rays," but it is not clear just what he meant by cosmic rays. Some scientists say that it was an early solar panel. But Tesla said that this device would work 24 hours a day. So it didn't require solar radiation, but some kind of, as he called it, "Cosmic Rays." There's an illustration of this patent in my book *The Lost Journals of Nikola Tesla*.

Tesla's patent refers to 'the sun, as well as other sources of radiant energy, like cosmic rays.' That the device works at night is explained in terms of the nighttime availability of cosmic rays. Tesla also refers to the ground as 'a vast reservoir of negative electricity.'

Tesla was fascinated by radiant energy and its Free Energy possibilities. He called the Crooke's radiometer, a device which has vanes that spin in a vacuum when exposed to radiant energy 'a beautiful invention.' He believed that it would become possible to harness energy directly by 'connecting to the very wheel-work of nature.' On his 76th birthday at his yearly ritual press conference,

Tesla announced a 'cosmic-ray motor' when asked if it was more powerful than the Crooke's radiometer, he answered, 'thousands of times more powerful.'

In 1901 Nikola Tesla was one the first to identify "radiant energy." Tesla says that the source of this energy is our Sun. He concluded that the Sun emits small particles, each carrying so small of a charge, that they move with great velocity, exceeding that of light. Tesla further states that these particles are the neutron particles. Tesla believed that these neutron particles were responsible for all radioactive reactions. Radiant matter is in tune with these neutron particles. Radiant matter is simply a re-transmitter of energy from one state to another.

Tesla saw that profits could be made from radiant energy, but somewhere along the line he had pointed out to him the negative impact the device would have. In an article for the June 1900 issue of *The Century Illustrated Monthly Magazine* where he described his new device he wrote: 'I worked for a long time fully convinced that the practical realization of the method of obtaining energy from the sun would be of incalculable industrial value, but the continued study of the subject revealed the fact that while it will be commercially profitable if my expectations are well founded, it will not be so to an extraordinary degree.'

CONTINUING TESLA'S WORK

Of course a lot of garage mechanics have been working on trying to perfect this and other types of Tesla-based Free Energy devices. Every year we hear reports coming from these people, and then the depressing results when these people try to get backing for their devices, try to get it patented etc. There have been scientists and inventors who have claimed that they've actually perfected or at least made working models of some of Tesla's Free Energy devices, but the information soon ends up being suppressed in various ways

Naturally, some of these accounts are going to be fraudulent. There's a number of people out there who are all too willing to make money off of gullible people by making extraordinary claims about Free Energy devices. But there are others who continue to work on Tesla's original theories. And hopefully, some day, we'll be able to actually hook ourselves into a machine that picks up energy right out of the ether so to speak. And we will no longer be dependent on fossil-based fuels and the evil cartels that have grown up around them.

CHAPTER SEVEN
THE MARS/TESLA CONNECTION

Having established the historical background and public achievements of the legendary inventor, the interview with Tim Swartz next moves on to an engrossing discussion of just how Nikola Tesla may have teamed up with various secret entities to actually lead man to the Moon and Mars decades sooner than we were ever told. Swartz again provides a wealth of detail and paints such a realistic picture of the tantalizing possibilities that there is little room for doubt that something vitally important really did happen behind the closed doors of Tesla's genius.

SWARTZ AND MICHAEL X

Question: Well, let's talk about Tesla and the Mars connection, which is the real thrust of this book.

Swartz: Let's start a little bit with my own investigation into the Tesla/Mars connection. You know, this was something that I first heard rumors about back in 1973. It goes that far back. I had read a book written by an author named Michael X that was published by Gray Barker's Saucerian Press. The book is still in print and is called *Nikola Tesla: Man of Mystery*.

That was the first book that I ever read where I'd ever even heard of Nikola Tesla. Which just really goes to show you how inadequate our educational system is. I mean, here was a guy who after he died, was awarded the patent for the invention of radio. Most people are taught that Marconi was the inventor, but it actually was Tesla. Marconi's radio experiments were all based on Tesla's patents.

So when I read this book by Michael X, it really opened my eyes and I wanted to know more about this Tesla. So I wrote to the author, and we corresponded a bit. In one of his letters to me, Michael X made a reference to Tesla's interest in the planet Mars. Michael X said that he had heard that Tesla had somehow been involved in a project that consisted of trying to send a spacecraft to Mars. Now when I first heard this story, it sounded very farfetched to me. It still sounds rather fantastic.

A PUZZLING STATEMENT BY DR. HYNEK

But through the years, I've heard other very similar stories from different sources. I next heard about the idea of a Tesla/Mars project, as I've come to call it, from the late J. Allen Hynek [the Air Force's public spokesman on UFO sightings]. In 1984, I was working at a television station in Dayton, Ohio, which is the location of Wright-Patterson Air Force Base. That year, the Air Force Museum opened a very small exhibit about Project Blue Book. And when I say exhibit, I mean it was a little glass case with a few pictures and a copy of the final published paperback book. It was almost laughable. But when they opened this exhibit, they had J. Allen Hynek come over and give a talk in the museum's auditorium.

So I got the chance to interview Hynek for the local newscast. At the end of the interview, as I was packing up the camera and gear, we were talking about television technology and how things work, and we got to talking about Tesla and his involvement in developing what would later become television.

Hynek brought up the subject of the Tesla/Mars project. And I was like, "What?" And he told me that there were files in the Air Force that talked about Tesla's attempt to send a spacecraft to Mars. Now that was all that he knew about it. But he had heard, from what he said were reliable sources, that Tesla had been involved in a project that involved a group of wealthy men from the East Coast that was building aircraft in the middle and late 1800s. And that these aircraft were what was being reported during the "flying machine flap" that started in California in 1896.

Hynek told me that this was one of the reasons that the United States government confiscated Tesla's notes when he died. That and Tesla had been saying that he had invented a Death Ray, and had tried to sell it to the highest bidder. He wanted the United States to have it, but the United States wasn't interested. And some other countries, including the Soviet Union, had expressed interest. So when he passed away, his notes and papers were confiscated by the government. And Hynek said a lot of it ended up at Wright-Patterson Air Force Base and there was continuing research being done with it.

SEANCES AND A SECRET SOCIETY

So from that, and other sources, I have been able to glean more details on the Tesla/Mars Project. Now I have to tell you that this is a story that I can't confirm or deny. I don't have solid pieces of a flying machine or anything like that. It's a really great story, but I can't confirm it. So I'm somewhat loathed to talk too much about it, but I really think that this book could help bring some people forward who may have more information about this.

What I've been able to gather is that there was a group of men in the middle to late 1800s, probably after 1850, who were receiving channeled communications from a spirit medium. Now the Fox sisters started the modern spiritualism in 1845. So this probably happened shortly after that. And it was popular during that time to hold seances and play with talking boards that were similar to what we now call Ouija Boards. People would sit around the table and they would have letters in a circle with a wineglass in the middle. And then everybody would put their finger on it and the wineglass would skitter back and forth across the table spelling out words.

A VOICE FROM MARS

Allegedly, it started out as a social club, and it could very well have begun with these guys wives getting together to talk to the spirits. They started to get messages from spirits, and eventually communication professing to be an intelligence from the planet Mars. These channeled messages then started feeding technological information that led to the development of early flying machines that this group put together and initially started flying in Northern California. This was what caused the spate of flying machine sightings that started in California and Washington state and then spread across the country. I know that in Indiana, Illinois, and Wisconsin, in April of 1897, there were a number of reports featured in the newspapers about sightings of the flying machines. And a lot of reports were quite consistent in that it was cigar-shaped with stubby wings and a bright searchlight.

MORE MYSTERIOUS VOICES

There was an article written in **FATE** Magazine in 1973 that talked about a club called The Aero Club that existed allegedly in California in the late 1800s. And in fact the author, Jerome Clark, said the club became a secret society, with the idea of developing a heavier-than-air flying machine. And I guess you're not going to come out and publicly say, "Well, you know, we got the plans for a flying machine from a spirit medium who was channeling an intelligence from the planet Mars." So they had to keep it very secret and locate funding from like-minded individuals.

What I next discovered was that in 1899, Nikola Tesla had built an experimental lab in Colorado Springs, Colorado. One evening, while researching the possibility of harnessing lightning for energy, Tesla became aware of strange rhythmic radio signals on his low-frequency radio receiver. He later wrote that he felt he was the first to hear the greeting of one planet to another.

When the newspapers picked up this story, the so-called Martian Messages created a firestorm of debate. No one had ever heard regular signals from space, and Tesla concluded that they must be from living creatures on a nearby planet, such as Mars.

What I have heard is that the Aero Club was also receiving these radio signals using a receiver based on plans that had been received from channeled information. They had no idea what they were listening to. They just knew this was supposed to be the proof that the channeled information they were receiving was factual and that the Martians were really out there. But they had no way to translate this stuff, if it was translatable. It was just meaningless noise to them.

TESLA JOINS THE CLUB

When the Aero Club read about Tesla's Martian Messages, he was contacted. And in fact there's a section in my book where Tesla talks about receiving a visit from some gentlemen that he thought were interested in backing his research. Instead they wanted him to put his name to psychic research, something Tesla had little respect for at that stage of his life. I suspect that this was the Aero Clubs first attempt at contacting Tesla.

Later, Tesla received financial backing from Wall Street financier J.P. Morgan. And I suspect that Morgan or at least somebody who ran in Morgan's circle was part of the NYMZA, the secret society that ran the Aero Club.

Tesla's mission was to help the Aero Club develop an aerial machine with a propulsion system that could fly them into space and onto Mars. Most likely Tesla considered this group to be peopled by suicidal madmen. But obviously after seeing the results of their earlier successful airships, Tesla could have been caught up in the enthusiasm of making such a grand project a reality.

If anything, Tesla saw the opportunity to continue working on his pet projects, like the wireless transmission of energy, with the money being supplied for the Mars Project. This was a situation that Tesla could not pass up, even if he didn't necessarily agree with the philosophy of this group.

The story as I have it was that with Tesla's help, the Aero Club actually made a craft that could fly based on what we would call "antigravity propulsion." Actually a better term would be "electrogravitics," which uses extremely high voltage electricity to create a lift. And Tesla was one of the first to propose this idea. In fact, there is an illustration with an article about Tesla in the October 1919 issue of *Electrical Experimenter* based on Tesla's description of a flying machine that looks very much like a modern-day UFO. It's like an elongated cigar shape. And this was a device that flew, based on energy received from a ground-based transmitter. And I think where this all ends up leading is that an attempt was made in probably 1903 to send this spacecraft to Mars.

FLY ME TO MARS

In 1901, with the backing of J.P. Morgan, Tesla started building what he said was going to be a world radio system on the East Coast in Wardenclyffe, New Jersey. Allegedly this was supposed to be Tesla's "World System," a central transmitter for wireless communication to relay telephone messages across the ocean; to broadcast news, music, stock market reports, private messages, secure military communications, and even pictures to any part of the world. However, this facility would actually serve several purposes. It would act as a radio transmitter, but it would also provide energy transmitted through space to the Mars spacecraft.

It is clear that Tesla was the right man for this monumental task. Supposedly the channeled instructions for building a spacecraft were technologically beyond the original scientists of the Aero Club. These scientists had been up to the task to build the first heavier-than-air flying machines years earlier, but they had no concept of the complexities of building a working spaceship, even if it was laid out right in front of them. They needed new blood, someone who was not afraid to consider the impossible, and Tesla was the man of the hour.

So it's just amazing to me that anybody could even conceive of this plan in 1903. But apparently something happened in July of that year, because residents around the Wardenclyffe facility reported strange activity. This was reported by **The New York Sun** on July 15, 1903. People were saying that they heard loud explosions. They saw huge bolts of lights and lightning "splitting the sky." And this massive electrical activity continued for some weeks afterwards.

TESLA'S FAULTY TOWER

The late conspiracy author Jim Keith, who knew of my interest in Tesla, told me through a series of e-mails that July 1903 was the launch date of the Mars ship. From a secluded location, the ship was lifted into the atmosphere using balloons and internal combustion engines. When it reached the desired height, Tesla switched on his "Magnifying Tower" at Wardenclyffe and sent a high-energy microwave beam to the receivers on the ship. The energy formed a bubble of ionized plasma that acted as a shield to keep in the oxygen and keep out the vacuum of space. The received electrical energy also provided the power to lift the craft out of the Earths atmosphere. The idea was that Tesla's tower was going to supply the spacecraft with the energy needed to send it to Mars.

It would be interesting to speculate on how many and who was on board this amazing ship. What kind of provisions did they bring and what did they think they were going to see even if they did make it to Mars. In those days' Mars was considered to be a likely candidate for intelligent life and popular literature would often portray Mars as a wonderful paradise, home to benevolent creatures, highly developed and of superior intelligence. But we have no way of knowing the thoughts and feelings of those on board because apparently, once it got out of the atmosphere, that was it. It was never heard from again. They had underestimated the amount of energy needed to power a craft all the way to Mars, and it was just too much for Tesla's Magnifying Tower to handle. Despite repeated attempts to contact the ship, it had completely vanished.

We do know that shortly thereafter, J.P. Morgan withdrew his funds from Tesla and the Wardenclyffe project was never finished. And in fact, in 1915, Tesla had to hand over the deed for Wardenclyffe to George C. Boldt, proprietor of the Waldorf-Astoria for outstanding debts of $200,000. Tesla was to never again enjoy the success of his early days and he was soon considered a charming eccentric, good only for amusing stories on his birthdays.

WAS THE MARS MISSION A PARTIAL SUCCESS?

By the time 1924 rolled around signals from Mars were a popular theme in newspapers and magazines, and when the orbit of Mars brought it close to the Earth in 1924, a well-organized program was set up to intercept any possible transmissions. Most of the major radio stations and ham transmitters around the world deliberately fell silent and listened.

Dr. David Todd, head astronomer at Amherst College, set up a device known as the Jenkins Radio-Camera at a naval observatory. On August 24, 1924, freak signals of unidentifiable origin were reported by listeners all over the world. Dr. Todd's apparatus produced a long strip of photographic tape that, when examined, displayed a fairly regular arrangement of dots and dashes along one side. According to *The New York Times*, the other side of the tape showed at evenly spaced intervals curiously jumbled groups of images, each taking the form of a crudely drawn human face.

This amazing experiment hit the headlines everywhere, and hundreds of amateur radio operators submitted reports of what they themselves had picked up. These signals continued to be received throughout the 1920's and 1930's with no explanation of their origin.

Nikola Tesla, who had grown increasingly isolated since his failed mission at Wardenclyffe, was excited to hear the news of the strange radio signals. He later reportedly confided to his nephew, Sava Kosanovic' who was employed by the Yugoslavian government, that he was certain the mysterious radio signals were from the lost Aero Club Mars spacecraft.

Tesla theorized the ship had indeed made it to Mars and was now signaling Earth to tell of their survival. This event spurred Tesla onto continuing his research and development of a radio transmitter and receiver capable of communication with other worlds. According to

Tesla's assistant, Arthur H. Matthews, Tesla perfected this device in 1938.

Evidence that Tesla had been seeking to establish radio communications with someone not of Earth came to light on his birthday in 1937. Tesla announced: 'I have devoted much of my time during the year past to the perfecting of a new small and compact apparatus by which energy in considerable amounts can now be flashed through interstellar space to any distance without the slightest dispersion.' (New York Times, Sunday, July 11, 1937.)

Mathews claimed that Tesla had secretly developed the Teslascope for the purpose of communicating with Mars. The late Dr. Andrija Puharich met with Matthews, and discussed him in an interview that ran in the May-June & July-Aug. 1978 issue of the magazine *Pyramid Guide*.

Mathews told Puharich that Tesla actually had two huge magnifying transmitters built in Canada, and Matthews operated one of them. People mostly know about the Colorado Springs transmitters and the unfinished one on Long Island. Mathews said he saw the two Canadian transmitters that were built to communicate with someone on the planet Mars. There's a diagram of the Teslascope in Matthew's book *The Wall of Light*. In principle, it takes in cosmic ray signals that are stepped down to audio. Speak into one end, and the signal goes out the other end as a cosmic ray emitter.

Matthews said that Tesla finally achieved direct communications with the survivors of the Mars project in 1938. It was revealed to Tesla that the ship had actually made it to the fourth planet because somewhere on Mars a duplicate energy ray was being sent out. The beam, identical to the one being sent from Wardenclyffe on Earth, had latched onto the ship and drew them in. And once they got to Mars, there was no one there. It was a dead planet. Apparently the radio signals that they had been receiving were from an automatic device that had been operating for God knows how long. There was nothing left living on Mars. Any intelligent life had been dead for a long, long time.

MARTIAN TECHNOLOGY, HUMAN UFOs

But apparently there was something remaining of Martian technology, because these people eventually came back to Earth using devices we now know as flying saucers. They may have returned in small groups as early as the 1930's. And then more often during WWII.

This is one of the dark secrets of the UFO mystery. Allegedly, our government is trying to keep hidden the fact that some UFOs aren't extraterrestrial, but are actually manmade ships flown by members of a secret society that has technology from a dead Martian civilization. They may have rejoined the group they left here on Earth. The group referred by C.A.A. Dellschau by the initials NYMZA. Or they may have taken over completely with their superior technology. If this is indeed the case, we must ask the questions: Are they bent on controlling the world? Why are they flying around in our skies in secret? What do they want? Someone knows, but they are not telling.

At this point, this is where the story becomes very nebulous and now it's just a lot of hearsay and rumors. But Tesla did have a number of his papers and notes stolen from him by German secret agents who were based out of New York before World War II. And the material that they were able to get from Tesla eventually led to the development of German flying saucers. And some researchers claim that the Germans actually went as far as to fly to the Moon and Mars, again, based on the technology that Tesla developed for the 1903 space flight debacle, or what at the time they thought was a debacle.

It's very interesting when you look at a lot of the early UFO contacts, especially those in the 1950s. The alleged aliens that were coming out of the flying saucers were almost always reported as humanoids, what we would call now the Nordic alien B but definitely human in appearance. Most of these UFO occupants could also speak English and seemed to have a good knowledge of our civilization. And have you also noticed that a lot of UFOs photos from that period have a 1950s look to them? They're very heavy duty, they almost look like they could have been produced at an auto plant somewhere. Some almost have cool tailfins coming off the back, which I find very interesting. If we consider that some group was building UFOs based on an alien plan, but still using an Earth-based technology, that would go a long way in helping to explain why UFOs seem to develop technically right alongside the scientific advancements of humankind.

Finally, I would like to put out a call for other researchers to help and try to add more information on this subject. I suspect that there could still be lost Tesla notes out there somewhere. If anybody else has heard similar stories, or maybe has some information that I haven't run across yet, I encourage them to write me at: commanderx12@hotmail.com

CHAPTER EIGHT ALTERNATIVE THREE, A SCIENTIST TESTIFIES

There is another route by which mankind may have reached the Moon and Mars many years before the times established in history as we know it. The fabled "Alternative Three" effort first revealed in the 1970s may have been successful in placing people on the surface of both of those distant neighbors in the sky.

WHAT IS "ALTERNATIVE THREE?"

Tim Swartz, in his book ***The Lost Journals of Nikola Tesla***, provides some historical background on "Alternative Three."

"At 9:00 PM on Monday, June 20, 1977," Swartz begins, "Anglia television, based in Norwich, United Kingdom, put out a one hour television special. The program was to be simultaneously transmitted to a number of countries, which included Australia, New Zealand, Canada, Iceland, Norway, Sweden, Finland, Greece, and Yugoslavia. The name of the special was 'Alternative Three.' It was to shock the nation, jam media telephone lines and rock the nation's credibility. At 10:00 PM Anglia was besieged with calls from irate viewers demanding more information. Callers were told not to panic, the program was simply an April Fools joke that had been preempted until June 20. However, many were convinced it was not a hoax."

And just what did the program have to say that so disturbed the viewing public?

According to Swartz, the journalists behind the program claimed that, "There is a secret joint U.S./U.S.S.R. space program that has gone far beyond what the public sees. Astronauts landed on Mars in 1962. It has been discovered that there is other intelligent life in the universe and they are observing and interacting with the inhabitants of Earth. The Earth is dying due to natural and manmade pollutants.

The increasing Greenhouse effect will cause the polar icecaps and glaciers to melt and flood the Earth. Extreme heat, such as that which is now inevitable, will melt land glaciers. That will result in a marked rise in sea level, and then there will be the start of extensive flooding B with London and New York among the first cities to be affected."

And so what is the solution, according to "Alternative Three"? There are actually three proposed methods of dealing with it, as listed by Swartz.

"Alternative One B Stop all pollution immediately and blow two huge holes in the ozone layer. This would allow excessive UV light to reach the Earth and millions would die of skin cancer. **Alternative Two B Immediately** begin digging underground cities for world leaders, the very rich, leaders of big business and a few selected scientists. The remainder of the population will be left to perish on the polluted surface. Alternative Three B Build spaceships and get the Elite off of the planet B to the Moon and Mars. Kidnap and take along some "ordinary" people for use as slave labor. Use mind-control techniques to control them. Leave the remainder of humanity to die on the planet."

No wonder the television audience was so outraged! They were being told that the vast majority of them were going to be deserted by their leadership and be abandoned to die soon after. While subsequent investigations of the claims made on the program never entirely cleared up the mysteries surrounding it, there are many who still believe the program was not a hoax but was instead a matter of cold, hard fact.

THE MOON, MARS AND THE ZETANS

One such believer in the truth of the "Alternative Three" scenario is a writer named John Winston, who posted a short but fascinating article on the website of *The Watcher* (http://www.mt.net/~watcher/nasamason.html).

Winston declares quite flatly that, "The 'Alternative Three' astronauts landed on the Moon and built their own bases many years before the Apollo astronauts landed on the Moon in 1969, as the result of a secret treaty between the Pentagon and the Zetans [obviously, Winston's name for the aliens]. The Zetans helped colonize the Moon with secret bases, and in exchange the Pentagon helped the Zetans colonize the United States with their own secret underground bases. The Pentagon decided that cooperating with the Zetans was a better idea than being invaded!

"The Zetans showed the Pentagon scientists," Winston continues, "how to construct nuclear and mercury powered saucers, as well as space shuttles, rockets and other NASA technology that was inferior to the antigravity magnetic-powered saucers of the Zetans and thus at a military disadvantage. Of course, our presidents did not want to go on the six o'clock news to talk about how they made a top-secret treaty with a violent, conquering foreign planet that in the past nuked Earth people. Not a bad reason for a big secret."

Once again, the Nazis become part of the overall picture.

"The Pentagon's secret saucers," Winston goes on, "were also aided by captured Nazi rocket scientists who were testing saucers they got from the Zetan instructors in 1944, when the Zetans had the Nazis do their genetic experiments for them, which was much easier than abductions. The primitive saucers, rockets, and shuttles of the Pentagon insiders, often mistaken for REAL UFOs, made it to the Moon and Mars."

DIFFERENT MARS, MOON LANDING SCENARIOS

The story Winston tells gets even more interesting.

"In May 1962," he says, "a secret spacecraft from the Pentagon landed on Mars and videotaped it. I have seen the actual video. It shows a Martian landscape far different than what NASA showed us! Mars had canals, lakes, green vegetation, swamps, and animal life on the surface. But NASA, the disinformation agency, wants you to believe it is a dead world so you will not expect extraterrestrials to live there. They have never shown the public most of the 2,000 photos they promised with Viking One.

"When the first Apollo astronauts landed on our Moon in 1969," he continues, "they were shocked to find it already inhabited. Thousands of Americans, Soviets, British, French and Australians were already living there. Astronauts who discovered too much truth and were considered security risks died in those famous accidents in the shuttle or on the launch pad, etc."

Were the warnings about "Alternative Three" meant to be heeded by those Ain the know?" Or is it more logical to assume that contingency plans like those described here do not exist? Should a major world cataclysm that required the removal of our leaders to safety ever finally happen, "Alternative Three" seems like a reasonable approach to dealing with it. Now if they only managed to include everybody else!

THE TESTIMONY OF ONE WHO'S BEEN THERE

Finally, there is the heartfelt testimony of Michael Relfe, who has posted a sizable book about his experiences on the Internet at: http://www.marsrecords.com. The book is free to the public to download and read.

As is often the case with an abductee, Michael Relfe only learned of his experiences years after the fact through the use of hypnotic regression. A biofeedback machine was also used to obtain accurate readings of the physiological effects of remembering his experiences.

UFO and abduction researcher Eve Lorgen conducted an interview with Relfe and his wife Stephanie that is posted on the same website.

In her introduction to the Q. and A., Lorgen writes, "Michael . . . . discovered he had been involved in a secret black project while in the Navy. Michael was astonished to find that he had been living a double life as a covert operative for the Mars Defense Force. Some of his assignments were covert ops, piloting spacecraft, remote viewing, psychic defense and even psychic assassinations.

"Michael's recruitment, training and service for the Mars Defense Force," Lorgen continues, "was carried out via sophisticated alien and military mind-control technology. This included implants, hypno-programming, dissociation of specifically trained alter personalities, advanced psi training, speed learning, psi enhancing drugs and time travel. Michael's case is unique and very important because he is one of the handful of persons who have been able to clear, recall and deprogram the sophisticated alien and military mind control programming.

"Michael still experiences abductions by an alien and human military element working conjointly. But because of his level of therapeutic success with deliverance, clearing and kinesiology, Michael has a greater sense of personal control and awareness, and is not as susceptible to the mind control that the abductors continue to try to use on him."

In other words, Michael Relfe was recruited and trained to perform various functions for the sake of a joint human-alien operation on Mars! And such was the extent of the mind-control involved that he did not consciously recall any of his "other life" as an operative of the secret Mars installation.

TIME TRAVEL "JUMPGATES" ON THE RED PLANET

At one point during the interview, Lorgen asked Michael about a part of the Mars operation called "Time Travel Jumpgates."

"I was not a jumpgate technician," Michael replied, "so I only remember things from a laymen's point of view. This technology was a result of the Philadelphia Experiment projects as described by Al Bielek. It's one of those things that are 'Oh, wow, fantastic' the first time you see them, and then they become taken for granted. I also remember that they were guarded really tightly and that every moment of use was accounted for and logged.

"I remember that there were several jumpgates on Mars Base," he continued. "These stations were 'hooked to' other places with gates and they were defended against someone or something. I remember that Remote Viewing technicians hooked to the machines assisted in that defense."

Michael goes on to enumerate two different kinds of people involved with the Mars facility.

"One is people visiting Mars temporarily," he explained. "Politicians, etc. They travel to and from Mars by jumpgate. They visit for a few weeks and return. They are not time-traveled back. They are VIPs. They are OFF LIMITS!! Second is permanent staff. They spend 20 years [as their] duty cycle. At the end of their duty cycle, they are age-reversed and shot back to their space-time origin point. They are sent back with memories blocked. They are sent back to complete their destiny on Earth."

The story of Michael Relfe is not only riveting in its own right, it also dovetails with other stories of human slave labor on the Moon and Mars!

THE FASCINATION CONTINUES

This has been a short survey of the many legends, rumors and folklore surrounding the belief that Free Energy and secret technology put us on the Moon and Mars decades ahead of when is normally believed to be the case. With the help of Nikola Tesla and the participation of Nazi scientists before, during, and after World War II, mankind may have made its giant leap long before Neil Armstrong's "one step for man" onto the surface of the Moon. Whatever the truth of the matter turns out to be, we can only be certain that the Moon and Mars will continue to fascinate us all as they beckon us to join them in the heavens.

Illustrations showing Tesla§s magnifying transmitter and electric
airships. Could this be the secret design of the
Aero Clubs Mars Expedition space ship?

CHAPTER NINE
COMMUNICATING WITH MARS

If Nikola Tesla was the only person on Earth claiming communications with the planet Mars, then his assertions would have to be greeted with skepticism until there was some kind or corroborating evidence. However, over the years, a number of other scientists and researchers have also come forward with their claims of Martian contacts.

In his article **Communicating with Mars: The Experiments of Tesla & Hodowanec**, Robert A. Nelson says that Tesla was widely criticized for his 1899 allegations of Martian Messages, yet no one could seriously dispute him, for he was a solo pioneer without peer. With the exception of the claims of Arthur H. Matthews, no one since then has reported constructing a Magnifying Transmitter or otherwise replicated his experiment, so the issue remains unresolved and the mystery unsolved. Tesla revealed no technical details in his pronouncements and publications of that period, other than the pertinent patents. His Colorado Springs notebooks were published in the 1980s, but they make no mention of his alleged contact with Mars.

Tesla elaborated on the subject of 'Talking with the Planets' in **Collier's Weekly** (March 1901): "As I was improving my machines for the production of intense electrical actions, I was also perfecting the means for observing feeble effects. One of the most interesting results, and also one of great practical importance, was the development of certain contrivances for indicating at a distance of many hundred miles an approaching storm, its direction, speed and distance traveled.

"It was in carrying on this work that for the first time I discovered those mysterious effects which have elicited such unusual interest. I had perfected the apparatus referred to so far that from my laboratory in the Colorado mountains I could feel the pulse of the globe, as it were, noting every electrical discharge that occurred within a range of 1100 miles.

"I can never forget the first sensations I experienced when it dawned upon me that I had observed something possibly of incalculable consequences to mankind. I felt as though I were present at the birth of a new knowledge or the revelation of a great truth. My first observations positively terrified me, as there was present in them something mysterious, not to say supernatural, and I was alone in my laboratory at night; but at that time the idea of these disturbances being intelligently controlled signal did not yet present itself to me. The changes I noted were taking place periodically and with such a clear suggestion of number and order that they were not traceable to any cause known to me. I was familiar, of course, with such electrical disturbances as are produced by the sun, Aurora Borealis and earth currents, and I was as sure as I could be of any fact that these variations were due to none of these causes. The nature of my experiments precluded the possibility of the changes being produced by atmospheric disturbances, as has been rashly asserted by some. It was sometime afterward when the thought flashed upon my mind that the disturbances I had observed might be due to an intelligent control. Although I could not decipher their meaning, it was impossible for me to think of them as having been entirely accidental. The feeling is constantly growing in me that I had been the first to hear the greeting of one planet to another. A purpose was behind these electrical signals!"

Decades later on his birthday in 1937, Tesla made this announcement: "I have devoted much of my time during the year past to the perfecting of a new small and compact apparatus by which energy in considerable amounts can now be flashed through interstellar space to any distance without the slightest dispersion."

Tesla never publicly revealed any technical details of his improved transmitter, but in his 1937 announcement, he also revealed a new formula, possibly pertinent to the apparatus: "The kinetic potential energy of a body is the result of motion and determined by the product of its mass and the square of its velocity. Let the mass be reduced, the energy is reduced by the same proportion If it be reduced to zero, the energy is likewise zero for any finite velocity."

L. G. LAWRENCE - COMMUNICATION BY ACCIDENT

In the 1970s, L.G. Lawrence (field manager of the Ecola Institute) described his communication by accident with ET intelligence's: "On October 29, 1971, while conducting exploratory RBS [Remote Biological Sensing] experiments in Riverside County, CA, our field instrumentation's organic transducer complex intercepted a train of apparently intelligent communication signals (tight spacing and discrete pulse intervals) while accidentally allowed to remain pointed at the constellation Ursa Major during a short rest period. The phenomenon prevailed for somewhat over 33 minutes.

"A somewhat similar phenomenon was observed on April 10, 1972. The apparent signals, aside from seemingly growing weaker, appear to be transmitted at great intervals ranging from weeks to months, possibly years. A faint, coherent, binary-type phenomenon was noted during aural monitoring. Intervals between rapid series of pulse trains ranged from 3 to 10 minutes.

"Because our equipment is impervious to electromagnetic radiation and found free of internal anomalies, the tentative conclusion of biological-type interstellar communications signals has emerged.

"As a mere audio presentation, the instrumentation tape is unpleasant to listen to. However, a fascinating degree of enchantment tends to emerge after the tape has been played back three or four times, typically over a period of weeks. We ascribe this to psycho-acoustical adaptation. The tape contains a short, incremental series of deep, harmonious oscillations resembling nonsense chatter or background modulations. An intelligent character of the overall pulse is applied by discrete spacing patterns, apparent repetitions of sequences, and highly attenuated Gaussian noise."

GREGORY HODOWANEC - GRAVITATIONAL SIGNALS

In the 1980s, electrical engineer Greg Hodowanec developed his theory of Rhysmonic Cosmology. He also experimented with a Gravity Wave Detector (GWD) of his own design. The simple devices detect 'coherent modulations' in the microwave background radiation.

Hodowanec published his first report of ASETI with Gravitational Signals" using his GWDs in the journal *Radio Astronomy* (April 1986): "The advantage of a possible gravitational technique for SETI over the radio technique is primarily one of time of 'propagation' for these signals. The radio waves travel at the speed of light, but the gravitational signals (per the writer's theories) are essentially instantaneous signals. Another advantage of the gravitational technique is the simplicity of the instrumentation required.

"As SARA members know, radio astronomy can be quite complicated. The gravitational wave detectors must rely largely on the Earth's mass as a 'shadow' to enable the detection of gravitational radiation. Therefore, objects or signals located in the observers zenith are best detected. Yet, the other areas are still 'detectable' especially with the aid of other 'shadows' such as the sun, moon, planets, etc.

"Of particular interest to SETI observers may be the strange audio type gravitational signals which appear to come from the Auriga and Perseus of our Galaxy. These signals have been heard by the writer for several years now, and generally range between about 4 and 5 hours right ascension, with a peak intensity near 4.5 hours R.A."

Soon afterward, Hodowanec made the first mention of definite contact with an apparently extraterrestrial communicator in a letter (7-23-88) to an editor at *Radio-Electronics* magazine: "On the morning of this date, at 7:30 to 7:38 "M (EST), I recorded the following apparently Morse code-like pulses:

"A"ARARTTNNNNKCNNNEEEEENENNTTTNEEEEEAEERKENNET EE"A"AEEENTTKNTNTSESESESEMNSESESESESESESESE

"As you can see, these do not appear to be just random pulses, but the SE signals, which are most prevalent, appear to be possibly an identification signal. These signals are detected in shielded l/f detectors and thus are scalar (gravitational) in nature. The signals above (if they were extraterrestrial) came from either the Auriga-Perseus region near my zenith or the Bootes region under my Earth position. I still cannot rule out that they may just be due to Earth core movements of some sort which are remarkably like Morse code signals, or even the possibility that they are man-made."

By July 1988, Hodowanec had confirmed Tesla's claims, as he announced in *Some Remarks on the Tesla Mars Signals* : "Such signals are being received today with simple modern-day scalar-type signal detectors... coherent modulations are being 'heard' in [the microwave] background radiation. The most prominent modulations being three pulses (code S) slightly separated in time, a la Tesla! On occasions, the code equivalents of an E, N, A or K are also heard, but the most persistent response is SE, SE, etc.

"Any l/f type noise detector will respond to this background modulation. However, the experimenter must be careful that he is not creating these responses at the 'local' level by his own or other local actions. For examples, the detectors will also respond to heart beats, breathing actions, local movements, as well as possible psychic effects. The detectors are easy to make and the experimenter should easily reproduce these results."

Hodowanec released more details in a **Cosmology Data Note I** (10-13-88): "Since about early August 1988, it was noticed that apparently 'intelligent signals' existed in these modulations [of the microwave background radiation]. It can be said that the intelligence was in the form of digital-type communication, e.g., dots and dashes, or ones and zeros. This type of communication may have been chosen by this 'unknown communicator' as if it was conducive to the 'mass movement' form of longitudinal gravity signaling, as well as an easily recognizable universal system. This same method was proposed by the writer for a gravity system communication method.

"These 'signals' were noticed to be similar to the simpler International Morse Code symbols, primarily because they are the simplest way to present information in the pulse form. Thus, the letters found in these transmissions are typically: E, I, T, M, A, N, R, K, S, and O, as well as the comma and the wait signal. However, the numbers are seen here as the simple series of pulses, e.g., one is one pulse, two is two pulses, three is three pulses, and so on.

"On August 26, 1988, after the writer had sent the message Greg Radio during a local gravity signal transmission test, it was noticed that the letters G and D were apparently added to some of the received messages noted thereafter!

"The writer's first hard evidence that the above test message may have been intercepted by this unknown communicator was seen that on August 28, 1988, a strong and repeated message of the Greg Radio was received with the message finally terminated with the series SE (or 31)!

"Further evidence that these may be actually communication attempts is seen in that on October 11, 1988, a very different approach was seen: A series of Greg Radio's was sent at about the normal code speed of about 5 words per minute, followed by KKTT, and then the series was repeated at a slower speed and also followed by KKTT.

"Another confirmation that these may be messages appeared on October 12, 1988. Here, a series of A's and R's (with Greg Radio occasionally inserted) was then followed by Greg Radio sent as a series of five repetitions of each letter, e.g., Greg was sent as **GGGGGRRRRREEEEEGGGGG**.

"Sufficient messages have now been received to indicate that perhaps a serious attempt to contact this writer was being made by some unknown communicator'. While this communicator may yet be some terrestrial experimenter, the possibility still exists that the communicator may be extraterrestrial for the following reasons:

1. The messages are in simple code (e.g., dits and dahs) type of pulses which would be expected to be used if one intelligent civilization were to try to contact another civilization in terms of pulses. That some of the simplest pulse signals are similar to simple Morse Code signals is more than coincidence – they are both based on the same premises!

"2. Numbers are not in the complicated Morse Code symbols, but are in simple sequence, using short pulses or dits.

"3. The communicator has recognized the coherent nature of Greg Radio and is possibly using that sequence of codes in various fashions to indicate that an intelligent contact has been made.

"4. The communicator thus far has not responded to word messages or the amateur Q- code signals. Thus it is believed that while some apparently Morse Code signals are being used, the communicator is not really familiar with such usage, other than recognizing the coherent nature of the signals.

"5. Since these messages at present appear largely near the noon hour, they may be coming from a definite source in space. At present, it is believed to be from the general direction of the constellation, Andromeda, but not necessarily the Galaxy there

"There is also some possibility that this communicator may be 'extraterrestrial', perhaps yet in our Solar System (Mars?), but no further than our own Galaxy or Local Group of Galaxies. Some communicator may have been trying to reach here ever since the turn of the century when Nikola Tesla reported the interception of scalar S signals!"

Soon after, Hodowanec wrote this brief, untitled report (3-13-89): "Without going into details of how this was determined: ET may be on Mars!

"This, in spite of NASA's denial of any life forms on Mars. This possibility has been recently suspected by the writer due to the apparently very close tracking of my position on Earth by ET. ET, of course, always knew that I was on Earth(as seen by his tracking), but now he has most emphatically confirmed that he is on the 4th planet from the sun, i.e., Mars!!!

"While this release is probably a bit premature, I am so positive of these gravity signal 'exchanges' that I will stick my neck out in this instance. ET on Mars is apparently much more advanced than we are here on Earth, and he may have even previously visited here on Earth, and possibly colonized here.

"It is still a mystery where ET may be living on Mars, and why ET doesn't use EM wave signaling methods? Perhaps, it is because Mars is so hostile now that ET must have developed a very sophisticated underground civilization which is not conducive to EM radiation systems?

"This material is being released now confidentially to a very few active colleagues until further confirmations of this assertion are obtained!"

In his *Mars Flash #1* (3-28-89) and #2 (3-30-89), Hodowanec notified colleagues of the following: "As the result of continued gravity signal communications between GH Labs and the Martians , the following extraordinary facts have come to light: The exchanges are now being made in terms of short 'English' code words for certain items. For example, the Martians now understand that FACE means the human face, MAN means the human person, Earth now means our planet, and Mars means their planet! They had originally tried some of their terminology on me, but gave up except where it made sense to me. For example, I know that **TTT** at the end of their names means person and **OOTT6AARR** is their name for the 10th planet!"

In a handwritten note to the above, Hodowanec informed this writer that the Martian's name is **AAAAAATTT**: "He appears to understand my messages, even though I may have to repeat them in several ways so that he can 'see' the meaning.

"Communications between GH Labs and a Martian intelligent now continue with increasing progress since we have been able to establish over 50 simple expressions (most in simple English) for many of the common 'ideas' that we have. Martian **AAAAAATTT** is extremely adept in relating my English terminology to these common Earth-Mars observations.

"Mars has also confirmed that they are also men with one head that have two eyes that see. Also they have two legs with two feet that have five toes each. I haven't been able to have them confirm the nose and mouth in the face, but that could be confirmed shortly, since those features appear in the face.

"Probably the most significant fact which was determined on this date seems to be that Mars is most emphatic that Earth men are like Mars men! It appears more and more that Mars has colonized Earth in the remote past! This could be true since we on Earth have never really found the missing link between Earth humanoids and humans!"

In a letter (3-17-89) to this writer, Hodowanec noted: "Generally, our contacts are limited to 20-30 minute, since there appear to be other ETs out there interested in joining in also, and so there is some interference after a while. Some of these other ETs use other methods such as tones and what appear to be guttural voices!

"ET is probably more advanced than we are on Earth. We no longer exchange simple arithmetic, and when I sent him Pi to five decimal places, he sent Pi back to seven decimal places immediately! We had discussed our nine planet solar system, but ET came back with ten planets, calling the 10th planet **OOTTAEERR**! When questioned on this, ET kept on confirming the existence of a 10th planet! He now knows the other nine planets by their Earth names! He also confirmed that Mars has two moons, the Earth one, and that Jupiter has nine major moons.

"These contacts are getting to be more interesting all the time, and ET appears to be most anxious to continue them. However, I just cannot spend too much time with him. I got across that I am just one person here communicating with him, and that the rest of Earth presently does not recognize the existence of any life on Mars.

"I have now had over 100 contacts with ET and can reach him at any time of day or night. We have also established some simple codes for acknowledgments and go ahead and respond. While we use these simple codes in many contexts, both ET and I now understand in which context they are being used!"

In another letter (3-22-89) to colleagues, Hodowanec affirmed this: "My contacts with a Martian intelligence has been advanced in a number of ways. The Martians are apparently an advanced civilization, for they are the ones generating the modulated oscillated beam which is now tracking my location on Earth and is thus the means of our communications. [The beam is "only about 15 miles in diameter here on Earth, but 10-12 inches on Mars."]

There is an apparent team on Mars which is involved in these contacts. The original contact, ET #1, with whom I established the initial relationship, is apparently the most highly knowledgeable and advanced. The others who sometimes man the Mars station appear to be less knowledgeable and some only request or acknowledge a transmission.

"Mars is most desperate to continue these contacts. The exchanges are made in many varied ways which cannot be readily predicted in order to convey the fact that these are real contacts! Also, one can recognize the fist of the one 'keying' these codes, e.g., ET#1 always sends clean letters or numbers, and identified himself and me in some fashion. The other ETs on Mars usually don't. Therefore, no automation is being used here.

"While these contacts were originally due to serendipitous circumstances, it is really the result of my gravitational communication experiments and thus a direct result from Rhysmonic Cosmology. And yet, however fantastic and unreal this may seem, it is real, and if also it is confirmed by one of you, it will be a major milestone in the history of mankind! Perhaps, if one of you finally hears the modulations of 1/f noise background, you may try to establish your own contacts."

However, Gregory Hodowanec also had extreme reservations about the gravity of the situation, which he expressed in a letter

(4-14-89) to Robert A. Nelson: "My contacts with Mars continue with much information being exchanged. However, due to the increasingly astounding nature of these exchanges, I am now limiting further releases to only two long-time observers (witnesses) of my research efforts. This is being done so as not to jeopardize these contacts with unwanted notoriety or publicity in the media. There are now nine *Mars Flashes* for the record. Perhaps, in the future, I may release some of these.

"Gravity signal communications are instantaneous, require extremely small energy expenditure, [unlike Tesla's experiments] and is so simple as to be just unbelievable by the average person. However, this is as far as I want to go with release of details at this time."

"I would appreciate that you keep this info somewhat confidential now. The Earth may not be ready for what I will have to say eventually. Nothing dire, just fantastic and thus perhaps unbelievable!"

It is interesting to draw parallels to the communications heard by L.G. Lawrence and Greg Hodowanec, to the alleged Mars Messages received by Nikola Tesla. The similarities are also evident to the channeled communications said to have been received from a spirit medium to the members of the 19th century Aero Club.

Another little-known member of the Martian Message club was William Marconi. In September of 1921, Marconi claimed to have received radio communication, from the planet Mars, on his yacht in the Mediterranean. At that time a radio transmitter could only transmit signals with a wavelength of up to 24,000 meters. Marconi's radio receiver picked up signals with a wavelength of up to 150,000 meters.

No transmitter was capable of doing that at this time and the regularity of the signals ruled out any possibility of electrical disturbances. The signals looked like a code. But the only part that could be understood was something which was similar to the letter AV in Morse Code. In New York by J.C.H. MacBeth, the London

Manager for the Marconi Wireless Telegraph Company, that the Earth was in the process of communicating with beings from the planet Mars.

Did these men receive 'live' communications from the planet Mars? Or, had they been fooled, like the ill-fated Aero Club's Mars Expedition, by a voice from a distant, long-dead past, forever calling out into the empty night?

Robert A. Nelson notes in his article that: 'Sometime later, Greg Hodowanec announced that he may have been fooled by a disincarnate entity. I do not believe that. Greg Hodowanec was a very careful experimenter, and well aware of the psychic aspects of his GW Detector circuits (as mentioned elsewhere in his writings). Even if that were so, then the Hodowanec G-Wave Detectors open a new door to the astral plane or parallel worlds. Some alien entities are known to utilize such interdimensional methods for communication and travel.'

CHAPTER TEN
THE RACE TO MARS

Mars has proved to be an irresistible draw for the adventurous and brave from planet Earth. Tesla's Mars Project may have been the first attempt for modern humans to reach the red planet, but it certainly wasn't the last. Even if Nikola Tesla didn't have the funds to continue developing the space technology he created for the Mars expedition B the original unknown financiers almost assuredly did.

Proof of this continued development can be found in the numerous phantom airship sightings that occurred worldwide after the failed Mars expedition. The secret group that funded the Aero Club did not stop their technological achievements due to one little setback, but forged on for their ultimate goal. Here is just a brief list of the many reported sightings.

1909 - A phantom airship wave visited New Zealand during this period of time as many people reported seeing boat-shaped aerial craft and lights-in-the-sky. During an encounter at Hawkes Bay in August, one of the occupants of an airship shouted out to a man below in an unknown tongue.

1910 - Arkansas: Myrtle B. Lee reported an experience she had with her brother when they were children in Fulton County Arkansas, 'We saw a bright object hovering just above the trees about 50 yard from us. It was silver colored and shaped like a Zeppelin, but not quite as big. It had nothing hanging from the underside and there were no windows. When it took off we saw it start up, and it completely vanished before our eyes. We called it a balloon. When I saw a real balloon, I knew what Jack and I saw wasn't a balloon. No one believed us when we told of seeing this thing.'

1910 -Alabama: Large cigar-shaped UFO hovers over Huntsville, Alabama and Chattanooga, Tennessee, playing its bright spotlight over both cities.

1912 - Illinois, Lockport: Witnesses watched, as an object appeared to traverse the moon's face for about three minutes. It was rectangular with absolutely flat ends, about two-thirds the diameter of the full moon in length.

1913 - Wisconsin: Large cigar-shaped UFO flies slowly over Milwaukee and Sheboygan, Wisconsin, flashing its bright spotlight over streets and buildings, and then retreats back out into Lake Michigan.

1913 - Michigan, Lansing: From The Lansing State Journal, June 30, 'So swiftly did the strange craft travel that it was not more than three minutes until it had passed from sight in the northwest. The aerial mystery carried no lights and was too elongated for an ordinary balloon. The craft was at a great height and when it passed to the northwest of the city had reached a still higher altitude.' Seen by a crowd at a racetrack in Lansing Michigan.

1913 - Canada, Toronto: Several office workers in watched what they concluded to be a fleet of airships passing west to east in groups. They then returned later in a scattered formation. No airships or airplanes were ever identified with this report.

1913 - England: Two years before Germany officially launched its Zeppelin raids on Britain and phantom airships were once again crisscrossing the night skies. A few reports gave details of multi-colored, multiple lights being seen but as in earlier years the craft usually came equipped with one powerful light. See Mystery Airships of Britain for further details.

1914 - Canada, Ontario: Eight witnesses saw a UFO floating on the water of Georgian Bay. Entities were manipulating a hose dipped into the water. On seeing the witnesses they returned inside, all except one who was still outside when the craft took off.

1914 - Norway: 'An airship might have been seen here at 8 o'clock yesterday morning December 20. Many reliable people, among them the sheriff of Solum, sighted the airship. The sheriff watched it with binoculars. It was at a dizzying height and moved first inland, but then turned southward and went away to sea.' The Morgenbladet, December 21, 1914

1914 - Norway: 'From Alta it is reported that Thursday evening September 17, from 9-10 o'clock a strange and so far unexplained luminous phenomenon was observed by many people and from many quarters. The sky was completely overcast and it was full dark when a luminous point like a very large star appeared to the east over Elvebakken, proceeded over Bosekop, disappeared behind Skoddevarre, came out again at Kvaenvik and after several other movements disappeared in the direction of Talvik. The light was white as a rule but shifted in part over to red and blue. It was also observed by binoculars from the small steamboat 'Sina'. Naturally it was guessed to be from an airplane. The light moved at various heights and as a rule without particularly great speed, except when it disappeared.' The Morgenbladet, Sept 24, 1914.

1914 - Norway: At Midlandet in Tjolta last Saturday evening November 21, an airship was seen again cruising about Skjaervaer Lighthouse, which it lighted up with a searchlight. The airship, which had a height of about 700 meters, descended to about 400 meters altitude, wherefrom it let the searchlight play on a passing ship. Thereafter it ascended again. Between 20 and 30 people watched it simultaneously.

1915 - Canada: It was billed in newspapers of the time as the Phantom Invasion of Canada. Mystery aircraft invaded the skies and capital of this nation.

1916 - Europe: 'A zeppelin-like object rose straight towards the clouds in the rear of our lines not like a flying machine, but straight up. After running vertically, it suddenly darted forward at a pace which must have been 200 m.p.h. It then turned around and darted backwards and then suddenly rising, disappeared in the clouds.' Maurice Philip Tuteur, a soldier on the British front during WWI, in a letter to his parents. The object was also allegedly witnessed by two sergeant majors.' The Morgenbladet, Dec 22, 1914.

1916 - Norway: Norwegian fishermen working nets north of Svalbard, Island see a 'dark Zeppelin' moving quickly over the Arctic pack ice, heading for the North Pole.

1916 - Ireland, Ballinasloe: A bright object was seen hovering in the sky. It was visible for fifteen minutes before traveling to the northwest. It was then observed to hover for a further forty-five minutes. It eventually vanished for good after Venus rose on the horizon.

1918 - Texas, Waco: Edwin Bauhan, one of several soldiers at Rich Field in Waco Texas who observed a 100-150 foot long cigar-shaped object after leaving the mess hall. 'It came directly overhead, and was no more than five hundred feet high so we got an excellent view of it. It had no motors, no rigging, it was noiseless, a rose or sort of flame color, I could observe no windows. We all experienced the weirdest feeling of our lives, and sat in our tent puzzling over it for some time.'

SECRET EXPERIMENTS

A contemporary of Tesla and the person wrongly credited as the inventor of wireless radio, Marconi was a mysterious man who publicly admitted to performing experiments in anti gravity aboard his yacht Electra. Marconi's yacht was a floating laboratory from which he sent signals into space and lit lights in Australia in 1930. He did this with the aid of an Italian physicist named Landini by sending wave train signals through the earth, much as Tesla had done in Colorado Springs.

In June 1936 Marconi demonstrated to Italian dictator Benito Mussolini a wave gun device that could be used as a defensive weapon. Marconi allegedly demonstrated the ray on a busy highway north of Milan one afternoon. Mussolini had asked his wife Rachele to also be on the highway at precisely 3:30 in the afternoon. Marconi's device caused the electrical systems in all the cars, including Rachele's, to malfunction. At 3:35 all the cars were able to start again. Rachele Mussolini published this account in her autobiography.

Mussolini was quite pleased with Marconi's invention. However, it is said that Pope Pius XI learned about the paralyzing rays and took steps to have Mussolini stop Marconi's research. According to Marconi's followers, Marconi then, after faking his own death, took his yacht to South America in 1937.

THE SECRET CITY

A number of European scientists were said to have fled to South America with Marconi, including Landini. In 1937, the enigmatic Italian physicist and alchemist Fulcanelli warned European physicists of the grave dangers of atomic weapons and then mysteriously vanished. He is believed to have joined Marconi's secret group in South America.

Ninety-eight scientists were said to have joined Marconi where they built a city in an extinct volcanic crater in the jungles of southern Venezuela. In their secret city, financed by the great wealth they had created during their lives, they continued Marconi's work on solar energy, cosmic energy, and antigravity.

Working secretly and apart from the world's nations, they built free-energy motors and ultimately discoid aircraft with a form of gyroscopic anti-gravity. The community is said to be dedicated to universal peace and the common good of all mankind. Believing the rest of the world to be under the control of energy companies, multinational bankers and the military-industrial complex, the story goes, they have remained isolated from the rest of the world, working subversively to foster peace and a clean, ecological technology on the world. Marconi's secret city is a common subject among certain groups in South America.

The French writer Robert Charroux in his book *The Mysteries of the Andes* (1974, 1977, Avon Books), says that tales of the underground city of the Andes is discussed in private from Caracas to Santiago. Charroux goes on to tell the story a Mexican journalist named Mario Rojas Avendaro, who investigated the secret society and their fantastic city and concluded that it was a true story. Avendaro was contacted by a man named Nacisso Genovese, who had been a student of Marconi's and was a physics teacher in Baja, Mexico.

Genovese was an Italian by origin and claimed to have lived for many years in the Ciudad Subterranean de los Andes. Sometime in the late 1950s he wrote an obscure book entitled *My Trip to Mars*. Though the book was never published in English, it did appear in various Spanish, Portuguese and Italian editions.

Genovese claimed that the city had been built with large financial resources, was underground, and had better research facilities than any other research facility in the world. By 1946 the city already used a powerful collector of cosmic energy, the essential component of all matter, according to Marconi's theories, many of which he had derived from Tesla.

In 1952, according to Genovese, they traveled above all the seas and continents in a craft whose energy supply was continuous and practically inexhaustible. It reached a speed of half a million miles an hour and withstood enormous pressures, near the limit of resistance of the alloys that composed it. The problem was to slow it down at just the right time.

According to Genovese, the city is located at the bottom of a crater, is mostly underground, and is entirely self-sufficient. The extinct volcano is covered in thick vegetation, is hundreds of miles from any roads, and is at thirteen thousand feet in the jungle mountains of the Amazon.

The French author Charroux expressed surprise and disbelief at the statement that the city was on a jungle-covered mountain that was 13,000 feet high. Yet the eastern side of the Andean cordillera has many such mountains, from Venezuela to Bolivia, spanning thousands of miles. Several such cities and mountains could exist in this vast, unexplored, and perpetually cloud-covered region.

Yet a secret city in a jungle crater was the least of the claims. Genovese insisted that flights to the Moon and Mars were made in their flying saucers. He claimed that once the technology had been conquered, it was relatively simple to make the trip to the Moon or Mars.

AL BIELEK AND THE PORTAL BETWEEN EARTH AND MARS

Al Bielek, noted lecturer on the famous Philadelphia Experiment and the time travel/mind control experiments of the Montauk Project has revealed that The Phoenix Project, the continuation of the Philadelphia Experiment was also involved in exploration of the alleged underground cities of Mars. The same ancient and abandoned cities discovered by the Tesla Mars Expedition in 1903.

With the success of the time portal projects, the Montauk researchers began to look off-planet for the next phase of Phoenix III. The idea was to create a portal between Earth and Mars. Specifically between Earth and the Martian Pyramids that lay near the great Face on Mars in the Cydonia region of Mars. It is said that this region of Mars shows evidence of a large number of artificial structures, including pyramids, the great Face, temples, a waterfront and even a city. It was the desire of the Montauk people to explore these structures and determine who (or what) had made them.

Part of the eagerness to explore these alien cities was the knowledge that the original Tesla Mars Expedition had returned to Earth in the early 1930's in spaceships built using ancient Martian technology. Using this incredible science, the UFOs being flown by this secret group were perceived as a threat to the existing world powers who eagerly sought advanced aircraft of their own to countermand the implied threat of the UFOs.

The crashed saucer at Roswell, New Mexico was one of the first Martian aircraft captured by the United States. This craft, which served as a reconnaissance vehicle to a larger mothership in orbit, was piloted by cloned humanoids who had been created specifically to pilot the UFOs. These creatures were cloned using ancient Martian science and with DNA taken from members of the original Tesla Mars expedition.

In order to fully explore the pyramids of Mars, the Phoenix III project needed to get inside the structures. This was accomplished by creating a time portal inside the pyramid and then move it around until open passageways were found. At this point away teams could enter the portal and walk from Montauk Point to areas under the Martian surface. Although little is know about what was found within this immense pyramid structure, a few tantalizing hints are offered.

Al Bielek says that Duncan Cameron himself was a member of at least one of the away teams, and described seeing something he calls "The Solar System Defense" which needed to be disabled before any further research could be done. What little actually remained had already been picked over by the Tesla Mars expedition.

AL BIELEK TALKS ABOUT MARS

In this exclusive interview, Al Bielek lifts the veil of silence and answers some direct questions about the Phoenix III project and what was discovered on Mars.

QUESTION: Since certain people in the know within the U.S. military had found out the UFOs were actually being piloted by earthmen using ancient Martian science, why did they start the myth that UFOs were extraterrestrials?

Bielek: Not all of the UFOs being sighted were from the Mars group. Some were actual ET craft that had been secretly visiting Earth for thousands of years. Maybe they were the descendants of the ancient Martians, we don't know for sure. But no one started an AET myth." It is just really impossible to keep a secret and eventually word leaked out that UFOs were spaceships with aliens at the control. At least some were.

QUESTION: Once the decision was made to open a tunnel to try and discover what the Tesla Mars expedition had uncovered, what did you find on Mars?

Bielek: Well I was not on the surface of Mars. We were in the underground. There are world government operations on the surface of Mars since about 1969. They are small operations really. After they were on the surface they found that there where entrances to the underground sealed and they knew there was something down there. The rumors were that there were probably artifacts from an ancient civilization buried underground because there were a lot of remains above ground, ruined cities, that sort of thing.

By NASA's estimates these ruins were maybe 300,000 years, 250,000 years old, and were probably part of the extinct Martian civilization discovered by the lost Tesla expedition. But NASA found the entrances all blocked, all scaled off to any underground areas. We knew the 1903 group had made it inside, found technology completely beyond our science and made it back to Earth. So we knew it could be done. So the word went back through communications back to the Montauk and Phoenix project, 'Can you do anything about this for us? We can't get into the underground of Mars.' They said, 'Yes, I think we can. Give us some coordinates on the surface of the planet. We'll have to run astronomical computation.' Which they did and plugged these all into the computer.

So they sent us and we went up there in the underground using the Montauk time-space tunnel device, developed as a result of the Philadelphia Experiment. We found eventually that the last remnants of the Martians, if you wish to call them that, died in the underground between 10 and 20,000 years ago by estimate, and they left everything they had of their civilization underground. The Tesla group had taken a lot of stuff away, but we found enormous amounts of statuary that appeared to be religious.

QUESTION: What did these statues look like?

Bielek: Typically six to eight feet tall with crystals and gems embedded in them.

QUESTION: Did they look human?

Bielek: Yes. The statues were quite well preserved. We also found archives and some scientific equipment. There were several authorized trips. And Duncan and I got the bright idea since everything was in the computer let's take a trip or two on our own and do our own exploring. So we did. After the second one it was found out and we were stopped. That was when he got into the archives and found enormous records of the civilization which was buried down there.

QUESTION: What did you find out?

Bielek: Duncan was the one that read them. I couldn't read them. He did tell me some things at the time but I can't remember any of it now. It's a very strange memory. On again, off again, and that part of it was never made clear to me as to what he really found. Right after that we were removed.

I do remember there were oxygen generators and they also had some storage. There was a generating system which apparently the ancients had left. I don't really know much about it. but it was activated before they moved the surface colonies in. They also melted down the polar caps. The rumors are that they used a hydrogen bomb or two for that. I don't know if that's true. But they did melt down a lot of the polar ice so they would have some water. It's still sparse but they have it. Some of the power generators are still working. After we turned on the underground lighting we had no lack of light.

QUESTION: The story of the Tesla Mars expedition was that members of the Aero Group were getting messages through a woman who claimed to be a spirit medium. The spirit claimed to be a living Martian sending its thoughts across space to Earth. The messages consisted in part on how to build heavier than air airships and eventually how to build a spaceship to reach Mars. As proof, the spirit told the group how to build a radio receiver to pick up intelligent RF signals from Mars. These were the same signals picked up by Tesla in 1899.

Bielek: The voice the group heard couldn't have come from any living Martian. We found none on the entire planet. The entire species is either extinct or left and never returned. But they did leave machines that could still operate. That's what the radio signal and the microwave energy beam that drew them to Mars were --automatic systems that somehow had turned back on. Maybe the Martians are still around-- not physically, but as spirits.

I remember the NASA telling us some years ago that they're receiving a low frequency radio transmission from Mars. It was about 50 kilohertz, if I remember correctly. Quite a low level indicating the equipment or whatever it was that was generating the RF signal, and it was coded and quite old. No one has been able to translate the message, if it even is a message. It could be a homing signal or something like that. But this is obviously the mysterious signals that the Aero Club and Nikola Tesla picked up all those years ago.

QUESTION: What were your impressions about being on Mars?

Bielek: We were digging in the remains of an old civilization that preceded ours and it felt very peculiar. To look at what was left, at what was once a great civilization and realize that they literally died there and left everything behind, it really humbles you and makes you realize just how fleeting our lives really are.

From what I understand of it, a number of the Martians survived whatever the attack was on the surface eventually took off for Earth and others decided to stay behind on Mars in the underground. And quite literally their progeny eventually died out and the whole race that was left behind on Mars died out. It's rather a strange feeling to realize that the remnants of a race died out in the underground totally. They just left all their hardware behind. That's all that remains.

CHAPTER ELEVEN
ANTIGRAVITY AND THE
NEW TESLA PHYSICS

Tesla speculated, that, perhaps the most valuable application of wireless energy, would be the propulsion of the flying machine, which will carry no fuel and be free from any limitations of the present airplanes and dirigibles. The possibility of electric flight intrigued Tesla and he pioneered research in what would later be known as Electrogravitics.

Tesla wrote in 1900 of an antigravity motor: "Imagine a disk of some homogeneous material turned perfectly true and arranged to turn in friction less bearings on a horizontal shaft above the ground. Now, it is possible that we may learn how to make such a disk rotate continuously and perform work by the force of gravity."

"To do so," he said, Awe have only to invent a screen against this force. By such a screen we could prevent this force from acting on one-half of the disk, and rotation of the latter would follow."

Does it not follow that such a gravity screen could also be used to levitate a vehicle? Tesla held no patent on such a device or on any other antigravity device. But if we are to believe that the Mars expedition really did take place, then Tesla most certainly played a hand in developing some kind of propulsion system that is only now being understood. After losing his financial backing, Tesla could not afford to continue his development of antigravity flight. He had hoped that he could come up with a system that could be affordable and mass-produced. But unfortunately, the complexities and cost of the system developed for the Mars Project made it unfeasible for commercial use. However, other scientists over the years were able to continue on where Tesla was force to leave off.

Edward Farrow, a New York inventor, reported in 1911 an antigravity effect produced by a ring of spark gaps. When the gaps were fired, the device, called a condensing dynamo, lost one-sixth of its weight.

T. Henry Moray wrote that frequencies may be developed which will balance the force of gravity to a point of neutralization. Antigravity researcher Richard Lefors Clark places the frequency of gravity's vibrations right at Nature's neutral center in the radiant energy spectrum, above radar and below infrared, at 10^{12} cycles per second.

Researcher Thomas Bearden, allows for gravity control in the physics he calls the new Tesla electromagnetic. Scalar (standing) waves in time itself can be produced electrically and this becomes a magic tool capable of directly affecting and altering anything that exists in time, including gravitational fields, says Bearden.

THE RESEARCH OF T. TOWNSEND BROWN

One person who carried on with Tesla's lost antigravity research was American physicist Thomas Townsend Brown. During the 1930's and 1940's, working with principles developed in association with Dr. Paul Alfred Biefeld, Brown succeeded in demonstrating that certain properly constructed devices, when energized with a strong D.C. potential could be made to exhibit a substantial loss of weight without an accompanying loss of mass.

Determined efforts to refine techniques and perfect methods finally bore fruit when, in the middle 1950's, Brown successfully flew, both in the air and later in a vacuum, electrogravitic disc-shaped airfoils powered only by high voltage direct current. These were demonstrated flying in 50 foot circles at speeds so incredible they were immediately classified.

The principle involved was one discovered by brown himself B namely that certain high-K (capacitance) dielectrics, when subjected to high-voltage charges in the 50 to 300 kilovolt range with constant input, will exhibit motion toward the positive pole.

Browns theory is that the capacitor is a useful tool in demonstrating the link between electricity and gravity in the same way that the coil is capable of representing the link between electricity and magnetism. He felt that given time as well as adequate funding and laboratory facilities, the problem of supplying the necessary electrical potential to the dielectrics of an internally transported power source while still enabling the craft to lift and maneuver efficiently could finally be overcome.

Project Winterhaven, which involved providing power to Brown's discs through a wire attached to the edge of the disc and tethered to a central pole which was connected to an external power source, looked exciting but proved to be one frustration after another as it somewhat inexplicably failed to attract either substantial governmental/military interest or the much needed money that tends to go with it.

Profoundly discouraged by an establishment that just didn't seem to care, quite possibly because their own secret research had been advanced to such a point that it had already surpassed Brown's privately funded efforts, Brown was eventually forced to abandon his efforts to build flyable hardware and to turn his talents to other more financially productive areas of scientific endeavor.

Even so, he never really gave up in his desire to discover a demonstrable connection between electricity and gravity. If large electrical potentials could be utilized to modify the local gravitational field, he reasoned, then certainly the opposite should be true as well. In an energy conscious world, any demonstration that gravity could readily be converted into usable electrical energy should have profound implications. All things considered, the work and discoveries of Nikola Tesla and Townsend Brown with respect to the apparent relationship between electricity and gravity are not only exciting, but absolutely fascinating.

TESLA PHYSICS IN THE 21ST CENTURY

A recent exciting development in the field of antigravity physics is with a few unassuming devices known as 'Lifters.' When charged with a small amount of electrical power, they levitate, apparently able to resist Earth's gravitational forces.

Currently, the devices can only levitate themselves. But developer Tim Ventura and others are working to convert electrical current into a force that can lift and move planes, trains and rocket ships. If that proves possible, the technology that powers lifters could extend the ability to explore space and drastically cut the use of fossil fuels on Earth.

Ventura, a UNIX programmer for AT&T Wireless in Kirkland, Washington, builds lifters in his spare time. He constructs the devices with balsa wood, aluminum foil and 30-gauge magnet wire. Ventura's lifters are triangle-shaped frames that at first glance looks like a box kite than anything else. But when connected to a power source, a lifter suddenly shoots skyward to the extent that its earthbound tethers permit, and then hovers about in the air.

Ventura uses an old Compaq computer display to power his lifters. Two wires come off the lifter, a positive power lead connected (PDF) via a high-voltage tap to the monitor's picture tube, which redirects electricity from the picture tube to the lifter, and a ground wire, also connected to the monitor.

Lifters seemingly do levitate and hover without standard propellants, but the problem is that no one is quite sure why. These devices are able to lift their own weight and they are modern versions of the Nikola Tesla and T. Townsend Brown Electrogravitic Apparatus. The Lifters are using the Biefeld-Brown Effect to generate the main thrust to self levitate. A basic lifter cell is composed of three Townsend Brown asymmetrical capacitors joined so as to form a triangle assembly.

Some developers believe that electricity stimulates the electrons on the lifter's surface, providing propulsion. Other theories such as ion-wind currents or electromagnetic disturbance of the air around the lifter have also been proposed, but there has been little scientific testing.

Ventura said he has considered submitting his work for scientific review, but it isn't 'on the top of my to-do list.' But he said he may soon be working with the Plasma Physicists project at Princeton University.

'I would welcome any real outcome to this research,' Millis said. 'Proof that lifters do or do not work would be equally valuable. Right now, all we have is what amounts to folk tales.'

Ventura readily admits that lifter developers do tell some strange tales.

One story is that the idea for lifters came from pieces of UFO wreckage taken from the Roswell site. A parcel of purported crash parts was sent by an unknown person to radio talk show host Art Bell in 1996. Bell sent them to a government researcher, whose investigations reportedly indicated that when electrical voltage was applied to the parts, they would move and in some cases levitate in much the same way as lifters do.

So some lifter developers believe that their devices are modeled after UFOs.

'As an inventor, I couldn't care less whether or not the idea for the technology came from a crashed UFO,' Ventura said. 'To be perfectly honest, I'm not what you would call a believer anyway.'

Ventura has tinkered with another lifter legend: the 'Gravity Capacitor.'

Said by some to be the true parent of current lifter technology, the Capacitor is rumored to have been developed accidentally by a 17-year-old trying to build a variation of 'Fitzeau's Condenser' (a type of energy storage device) in the 1930s, and instead stumbled upon a method for controlling gravity with electricity.

When the boy connected his tinfoil and waxed-paper device to the ignition coil of a Ford Model T, the Capacitor immediately levitated at such a tremendous speed that it left behind only a smoking exit hole in the roof of the barn.

Ventura wryly notes that the capacitor's self-destructive nature makes it a less-than-ideal test apparatus for investigating gravitational forces.

'Six hours of cutting foil strips and waxed paper is a lot of work for three seconds of smoke.'

Still, many researchers are intrigued by lifters and their potential. We could be looking at the first steps of a whole new science and economy based on antigravity rather than fossil fuels. If current scientists and even garage mechanics are not afraid to risk their reputations by undertaking such a 'forbidden' project, then lifters could be the humble beginning of rediscovery of the lost Tesla physics.

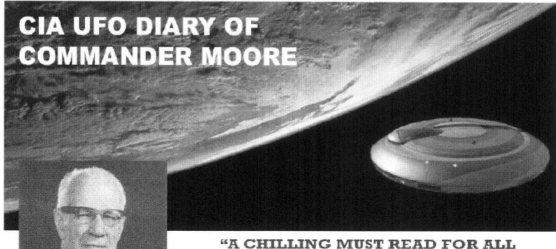

CIA UFO DIARY OF COMMANDER MOORE

"A CHILLING MUST READ FOR ALL CONSPIRACY PRONE UFO ADVOCATES"
TIMOTHY GREEN BECKLEY, EDITOR UFO UNIVERSE
A former Navy Commander and CIA operative's private memoirs involving the retrieval of wreckage from a UFO shot at over the Nation's Capital and how pieces of this craft were stolen from a safe inside a supposedly secure government office building in Washington, D.C.

REVEALED FOR THE FIRST TIME!

· How aliens he defines as *"Skymen"* have been coming to Earth's surface and exploring it for what could number thousands of years!

· Some of these beings possibly have homes in caverns on the moon, Mars, Jupiter, or the asteroids!

· Many more originate much nearer to the Earth's surface, from *"Skyislands"*, or even from within the hollows of our planet, and possibly underwater hangars!

· The *"Skyislands"* are apparently orbiting the Earth in several bands or chains, likely indicated by jet streams!

· *"Skymen"* have kidnapped a multitude of people and skycraft users have long extracted blood from surface animals and humans, and commit mysterious murders!

★ ★

NOW YOU CAN ADD THIS RARE BOOK TO YOUR LIBRARY!

THE SECRET UFO DIARY OF CIA OPERATIVE COMMANDER ALVIN E. MOORE EXPOSES THE EXISTENCE OF THE SKYMEN AND INVISIBLE PLANET X

Read the section in this book about the possibility of invisible worlds — or Sky Islands as Commander Moore called them — then order your copy of the amazing, 275 page, CIA UFO DIARY by Commander Moore for **$16.00 + $5.00 S/H**
Global Communications · Box 753 · New Brunswick, NJ 08903
Credit Cards: 732 602-3407 - Pay Pal: MRUFO8@hotmail.com

A Fascinating And True Story! A Classic From The Golden "New Age" Of Flying Saucers!

THE AUTHOR BEFRIENDED THE BEAUTIFUL LIFE FORM FROM ANOTHER WORLD ... BUT WAS SHE A SPIRIT OR A SPACE BEING?

Dana Howard had been a sensitive since childhood. While still a youngster, she was stricken with tuberculosis and told by specialists she had to undergo an amputation of a limb or suffer an untimely death. Guided by a power higher than childish reasoning, while still awaiting surgery, the young girl went on a hunger fast. Her frantic mother called in a new doctor. He offered little hope for recovery and refused to operate. Shortly after this, Dana's frail body was encased in a heavy plaster cast. It was then that her strange nocturnal travels out-of-body to more serene and beautiful worlds began. The child claims she even made friends in this "fantasy" realm.

When the cast was removed – revealing a complete miracle healing, the stuff of medical history in the making – she soon forgot her night wings. Later, the urge to fly returned, culminating in a flight by teleportation to the planet Venus. It was then that Dana Howard met the beautiful Venusian messenger who called herself . . . Diane. Later, the author visited again with Diane in the picturesque Mojave Desert, which she soon became aware was actually a portal between worlds. The desert was a lo-

An ectoplasmic form begins to materialize from the orifice of a medium, eventually to take the shape of a human. Was Dana Howard's contact with a spirit or a space being?

cale which had inspired many stories of UFO landings and meetings with extraterrestrials by such famous flying saucer pioneers as George Adamski, Orfeo Angelucci and George Van Tassel. The desert, it seems, was "alive" with spiritualized energy, apparently acting as a magnet, pulling the "Venusian" Diane from the ether onto the desert floor.

Dana describes how Diane sometimes seemed to slowly dematerialize and appeared to be sinking "into the earth." On these visits the materialized form would offer hope that humanity could get it together to better meet the intense challenges soon to come: dramatic climate changes, structural changes to earth's geography, changes to the world economy and society's infrastructures, as well as eerily prophetic warnings about the climate changes, pole shifts and economic fiascos we're currently experiencing – all foretold back in the 1950s.

Farfetched as her experiences may seem, something happened that added weight to her fantastic encounters. The author's inter-dimensional friend appeared not only to her,

Concludes on following Page >

but also to an amazed group of 27 people who had gathered with Dana Howard in a small white church in Los Angeles on April 29, 1955 for the purpose of conducting a séance.

Diane began to form out of a single thread of ectoplasm: "In my mind's eye," Howard writes, "I could still see those strings of milky white substance that reached almost to the ceiling of the church. I could still see the blue-white light behind the stringy substance. I had gained some knowledge of these alien plasmas in my Venusian experience."

This book contains a full update on this work by noted contemporary researchers Regan Lee and Sean Casteel, providing a number of examples of such ectoplasmic materializations caught with the eye of the camera in amazing and controversial feats of spirit photography.

Order *OVER THE THRESHOLD* now for just $20 and receive a 50 minute **BONUS Audio CD** featuring the beautiful enchanting voice of Mollie Gibson singing the folk songs of the Space Brothers. *FROM WORLDS AFAR*, orchestrated during the Golden Age Of Flying Saucers.

WANT TO LEARN MORE?

Don't miss another Dana Howard classic *UP RAINBOW HILL*...with its important messages of peace and love from the cosmos. **$20.00 or both Dana Howard books in this ad with CD just $35.00.** Add $5.00 to total order for shipping and handling.

> **Global Communications**
> **Box 753**
> **New Brunswick, NJ 08903**

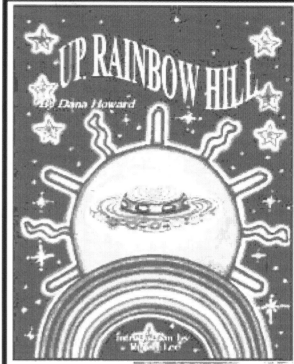

Dana Howard

UP RAINBOW HILL

$20.00 + $5.00 S/H if purchased alone.

—COLLECTORS ITEMS—
AN AUTHENTIC REPRINT OF A TRUE CLASSIC FROM THE GOLDEN AGE OF FLYING SAUCERS WITH BONUS MUSICAL CD OF AUTHENTIC 'SPACE BROTHERS' FOLKSONGS

DANA HOWARD'S SPACE CONTACT WAS A BEAUTIFUL, BLONDE, EIGHT FOOT TALL WOMAN WHO MATERIALIZED IN FRONT OF A ROOMFUL OF PEOPLE